Dads, Kiss Your Sons

Dads, KISS YOUR SONS

MARK CRAVEN

Cover photo by Jamar Cromwell (IG: @evoke.create)
Cover formatting/design by Danna Mathias Steele
Copyediting/project direction by Grammargal on Fiverr

For Kai—you've shown me levels of love I could have never known without you.

"Life is not a private affair. A story and its lessons are only made useful if shared."

—Dan Millman

INTRODUCTION

It's probably a good thing that I caught the inspiration to write something like this. I'm a big guy, I have a lot of tattoos, I sang in a death metal band, and I worked as a bouncer for a while. Now, I don't say all of that to prove that I'm some kind of badass, but I do look the part of someone you might not want to fuck with—at least initially. Because of that, when I say to dads, "You should hug and kiss your sons," those traits play in my favor because they're less likely to think I'm some wimp and actually hear me out.

Looks can be deceiving, however, and I don't want all of this bravado to fool you or sway your thinking too much—I know nothing about sports, my absolute favorite pastime is sitting in a café drinking coffee and reading, and I like musicals. To be honest, my taste in music ranges from Cradle of Filth to Josh Groban.

Men are afraid to admit things about themselves that they believe will somehow make them appear as weak. Who they're concerned is judging them in this way is a mystery, but they do it—we all tend to do it until we realize how foolish it is. When I lived in Los Angeles and told people that I wasn't into sports, they were mortified. "How can someone who looks like you be from Pittsburgh and not be a raving Steelers fan?" It's just not part of me, it's not something I've ever really given a shit about. Music, though, and coffee, and books—now you're speaking my love language.

Wait, wait, did this six-foot-tall half-black guy with a neck tattoo just say the words, *love language*. See, those are the natural perceptions that our culture has imposed on us. Someone who looks like me and isn't gay can't possibly be into the things that I'm into. And gay men can't possibly like sports either.

I have a good friend that I met—you guessed it—not at a Steelers game but in a coffee shop several years ago. He and I saw each other in the same café often enough that we started talking one day. It was a few years after we'd met and established a strong friendship that he said to me, "Ya know, when I used to see you in here, before I knew you, I thought you were an asshole. You just looked like some big puffed-up asshole. But I was wrong."

I loved that conversation, and I'll hold onto it forever.

If you're reading this and you are a sports fan, this isn't an attack on you. You should fully like and embrace what you like and embrace, and if it breaks away from your societal structural role as a man, let that be OK. I don't like sports; I didn't say I don't like you. The point is, I look like someone who should, and I don't, and that's OK. It's OK that you like the "not-so-manly" thing that you like too. Just like it's OK for me to not like the 'manly' thing that I don't like.

―――――

I met my dad when I was twenty-two. His name is also Mark. He turned out to be a great guy and offered me a chance to move in with him and fund my college education should I choose to go. At that point in my life, my band was kind of hitting a wall where some of us wanted to take things to the next level and others wanted to stay where they were. One thing about being in a band is, if everyone isn't on the same page regarding taking chances and running after the same dreams, one person can't do it alone—hell, two people can't. If there are five people in your band, you need five people to want the same thing just as bad in concert with one another (pun intended).

I started to realize that I needed to go back to school right before I met my dad. Along with pushing my rockstar aspirations, I was working on an ambulance as an EMT and delivering pizza. I hated the jobs I was doing and made my mind up that I was going to go back to school. A few weeks later, I met my dad. The Universe does crazy things when you make your mind up about something.

Not only did he offer me this chance to begin my college education, but he also lived in what looked like a damn castle and invited me to live with him and his family. At the time, I was living in the same rundown city I was born in, with five roommates and a collapsing ceiling in my bedroom—literally a gaping hole in the ceiling with crumbling plaster that would fall and cover my bedroom floor every few days. I'm surprised that I never had a bird or a bat fly in and attack me. So when my newfound dad opened the huge wooden doors that led into the biggest house I'd seen up to that point in my life, I was more than willing to hear him out on why I hadn't seen him those last twenty-two years.

My mom and I have a terrible relationship. We've never gotten along, and to this day it remains a struggle to have a simple conversation with one another. I'll get more into this story later, but to touch on it briefly now, she's had untreated mental health problems all her life, and one of her greatest afflictions is being a pathological liar. An example of her mythomania that had gotten back to me was that she told her coworkers that her husband had been killed in a car accident by decapitation and she had gotten stuck raising his biracial son. My mom had never been married, and when I was little, if anyone even thought about asking her if I was biracial, she'd lose her mind on them and go fucking ballistic, solidifying her racist stance. This remark also shows that she never really wanted to take ownership of me as her son—that's been a lot of fun to unpack as an adult!

Because of the home I grew up in until I was fifteen, which was when my mom moved to California and I stayed in Pittsburgh, moving in with my aunt Doe (the best person I've ever known), I've been overly aware of the importance of mental health—talking about it, advocating for it, and seeking help for my own. I took a lot of insecurities, anxiety, and depression into my adult life that began when I was a little kid—a result of my mom telling me we were doing something fun the next day only to not deliver on the promise, and doing this over and over and over and over and over.

Because it happened so often, being let down became commonplace. I just assumed that no matter what, I would always be let down. Trust wasn't even an option because this persistent letdown was a consistent inevitability. That was my thinking in second grade. I can look back now on this with understanding and forgiveness, but as a child I couldn't—so those scars dug pretty deep. I made a vow in second grade to never get my hopes up or excited about anything because I was always let down—seven years old with such grim expectations of the future.

I understood who my mom was before my dad, Mark, ever had to tell me that she wanted him and his family as far away from me as possible. I believed him because my own family, my mom's own family, had told me the exact same thing as I was growing up when I'd ask why I didn't have a dad. "Your mom just decided she didn't want him around you at all, and she was hellbent on ripping you out of our lives, too, if we took you around him," often was what I was told as I got older. There was never really a clear reason for her doing this aside from her standard unpredictable outbursts of anger, rage, and other illogical and unfounded actions—there was a time that she swung a hot iron at me. The timing was like a movie, as the steam blew out of the iron just as she stopped a few inches short of my face.

The reason?

She asked if I had finished my cereal but didn't believe me when I said I did while holding the empty bowl. I was maybe twelve or thirteen when that happened.

But after meeting my dad, I was soon to find out why she may have made this decision to keep him away from me all those years ago. Not to excuse her episodes of randomness and rage, but this new knowledge may have had something to do with her motives.

Three years after meeting my dad, he wanted to put me on his health insurance, but his company needed us to do a paternity test because we have different last names. The test came back negative . . .

After three years of living with my dad, having finished an associate's degree and now working toward a bachelor's, we came to learn that he wasn't my real dad. He was devastated. I was unsurprised because I had known my mom for a long time, and this was something that could easily fall out of her playbook.

For me, nothing had changed between my dad and me, but for my stepmom, they had. She thought that I knew the whole time and that I was taking advantage of the situation—though if that were true, it seems unlikely, at least logically, that I would agree to a paternity test that would surely ruin this good thing I had going.

No, it was simply, as I said, that I knew my mom. And at that point in my life, nothing from her came as a surprise or shock to me. It's unfortunate to have someone in your life that you plan for and expect the worst from, and they never let you down in that regard, especially when it's your mom—and especially when they do let you down in every other regard to the point that you become a seven-year-old in second grade who totally dismisses the possibility of hope from his life.

I don't write all of this to bash my mom. She had untreated and undiagnosed issues going on, was working full-time as a single mom, and had put herself through nursing school. She wanted to give her son more than she could, and that's where the empty promises came in. She did love me and wanted to love me better but likely didn't know how to—it's very hard to function at what would be your optimal or even suboptimal state when you're battling a daily inner war with your mind. This is especially true when you're isolated in the battle and doing it alone without the right help. So, in writing this, I'm not bashing my mom; I'm telling the story of the things that have happened in my past between us that are why I now have to look back on that past with understanding and forgiveness.

That kind of sounds noble, but let me assure you that it's more difficult than I'd like it to be. My blood still tends to boil when I'm on a phone call with her, and it's a daily practice to not ruminate on things that would feed the flames of unforgiveness toward her. The problem with the flames of unforgiveness is that they burn the shit out of you, while the flames of forgiveness burn off the chains that keep you bound to the wretchedness of the situation. That sounds good, but it isn't easy. And that's OK—we've just got to do our best.

Not long after the results of the paternity test came back, I moved out of my dad's house, but I continued my education, and today I have a master's degree from the University of Pittsburgh. I'm not sure that would have been possible if I hadn't met the person I thought was my dad when I was twenty-two—though he tells me that I still would have gone back to school and finished my degrees even if we hadn't met. He and I do still go out for breakfast on weekends, and I still call him Dad. He says that I would have gone back to school without him, and he's probably right, but he was instrumental in showing me that obtaining higher levels of education was possible, because he had done it. He came into my life at a perfect moment when I desperately needed to see an example like that. Would I have gone back to school without him? Likely. Would I have gone back to school with the same level of hope and belief without him? Unlikely. Did that hope and belief help me achieve the levels of education I've achieved? Undoubtedly. Thanks, Dad.

I found out that my real dad, my biological dad, was previously a wrestler in the WWE (WWF at the time that he wrestled). It was my older cousin, Vicky, through tears after I told her about the paternity test, who explained to me that my mom was seeing this other guy around the same time she got pregnant with me. She told me to look up the wrestler, and with a simple search of YouTube, I found a wrestling match that made it look like I had somehow transported myself to 1983—we looked *that* similar.

There was absolutely no question about it. Mark, who I thought was my dad, lived with for three years, and was named after, was not my dad. Mark is also Italian, and that's the ethnicity that I thought I was for so long—twenty-five years to be exact. Instead, my dad was this guy in wrestling trunks being thrown around a ring in the 1980s WWF. And he was black.

Dads, kiss your sons. What does that mean? It means exactly what it says—show love and affection to your sons. Let them know that love is more than a word and that it can absolutely be felt and that it should absolutely be felt. Kiss your daughters, too, but the point of kissing your sons seems to be one that's lost to our overly masculine societal way of thinking about what it means to be a man.

I've kissed Kai, my son, relentlessly since the day he was born. He has no say in it and I'll never stop. I hope these next pages can open more men to feel comfortable in who they are and show them the importance of kissing their sons. I'll use stories from my life, peer-reviewed articles to get into the scientific literature underpinning my posits, and various self-development strategies that will bring you to the fullest version of yourself so that you can love your son in the fullest way possible.

If you don't read any further than this introduction then let me just say this: Dads, kiss your sons. Everything else will fall into place as it should, but, please, kiss your little boy. Beautiful healing awaits you in this process, and beautiful hope, security, and strength await your son.

The stories shared in the following pages are meant to inspire hope and change in you, real change that will make you a better man and father. I believe you'll find healing. I believe you'll find hope. I believe you'll find all that you need to find.

1

STEAK KNIFE MEMORIES

My mom and our relationship begin here. One of my first and earliest memories was seeing her in a screaming match with my grandmother. It ended with my mom going into the kitchen, grabbing a steak knife, and cutting her own wrists in front of us, screaming, "IS THIS WHAT YOU WANT?"

My grandmother was fast to grab the knife and throw it into the sink—I still clearly remember the sound of the knife hitting the steel tub and clanging around. I still clearly see the shallow, partial lacerations on my mom's wrists. She didn't cut very deep, and you can't see scars on her wrists today, but the impact that it had on me was something that I've never forgotten—obviously, since here I am more than thirty years later talking about it. I guess I was somewhere between three and five years old.

This was a first memory. This was a formative memory.

We can't help the homes we were born into, and many of our childhoods are scarred like this—often much worse, or not as bad, but scarring is scarring, broken is broken, and your pain is valid. We do, however, have a significant degree of control in the homes that our own children are born into. I hope that one of Kai's first and formative memories is me doing wrestling moves on him, followed by tickling him into a laughing oblivion (after all, wrestling is in our blood). Or watching Pentatonix videos with his mom. Or being smothered every day in a relentless barrage of kisses and hugs. Or sliding down the stairs on his belly. Or falling into random fits of laughter when I and his mom kiss each other—which has kind of given me a complex, like, am I a bad kisser? What the hell is he laughing at? Or . . . Or . . . Or . . . fill in the blank with anything that builds his security and joy in knowing how loved he is.

Dr. Bruce D. Perry writes, "During the first three years of life, the human brain develops 90 percent of adult size and puts in place the majority of systems and structures that will be responsible for all future emotional, behavioral, social and physiological functioning during the rest of life."[1]

Much of the brain's biological structure and neurological connections are established within the first three years of life. That's mind-blowing and should put into perfect perspective just how critical it is to take advantage of those first few and, let me add, very fast-moving years of our children's lives.

In creating an environment of stress, worry, fear, and trepidation, those are the established and strengthened emotional wirings that the brain is programming. In creating an environment of love, support, security, and laughter, those are the established and strengthened emotional wirings that the brain is programming and making the child familiar with.

What a beautiful life to be unfamiliar with fear—or at least less familiar with the emotion of fear than you are with the emotion of security.

While this infant gazes up at you, your loving or unloving actions tell his brain a story. And that story is what his brain will tell him for the rest of his life.

The story is either that you're loved, protected, and deeply cared for, or you're a burden, there's another place and something more important to me than you, and you're not deeply loved or cared for. That second story, especially when I think about my own child, breaks my heart.

My son Kai's emotional and behavioral disposition have almost everything to do with how his mother and I show him that he's loved—both how we show it to him right now and how we've shown it to him these last two years since he's been born. Words are wonderful and hold incredible power and should be spoken even to an infant. But words don't wrap the infant in warm arms, triggering the release of neurotransmitters that calm him and decrease the presence of neurotransmitters that would stress him. Kissing his forehead and his cute little face allows him to feel what you mean when you say those strange murmurings he hears of, "I love you."

Dr. Perry goes on to say, "Without predictable, responsive, nurturing, and sensory-enriched caregiving, the infant's potential for normal bonding and attachments will be unrealized. The brain systems responsible for healthy emotional relationships will not develop in an optimal way without the right kinds of experiences at the right times in life."[1] Notice what he said here—"sensory-enriched caregiving." This is exactly what I mentioned above. Sensory enriching is when your baby feels you, is close to you physically, is tickled by your stubbly chin, and experiences this in a predictable way.

A predictable way, as Dr. Perry mentions, means that your son knows that when he hears your voice or sees you, he is going to be picked up, held, hugged, kissed, and cared for. This creates a deep sense of security within him. This creates a knowing that he is loved that is unalterable. There's nothing I want more for Kai than for him to know how deeply and unconditionally he's loved. There's nothing he can do or not do that will determine how covered in unchanging love he finds himself every day. With this knowing, he will become secure not only in my love for him but also in who he is becoming. Fear will diminish. Courage and daring will be his allies as he gets bigger and starts new adventures beyond being an infant—like climbing all the furniture in the house, climbing me and doing backflips from my shoulders, or, as he keeps getting older, realizing that any dream he has is possible.

A therapist I used to see, probably around the time that I was twenty-five, explained an interesting exercise to me. I shared with her that I held deep insecurities, and they especially shined through when I was in a relationship with someone. No matter who I was dating, I could never overcome the trust barrier. I always assumed the other person would cheat even though I'd never been cheated on up to that point nor had that person done anything to give me an inclination that they would cheat. It was just lodged in my mind that this would happen.

It was the insecurities that I brought into adulthood that fed these illusions. It was that decision I made in second grade to never get my hopes up and to always expect the experience of letdown. Along with this, my mom would often comment about my weight and acne as I was growing up. She would always say that I was fat and needed to work out more—even though our dinner plans would usually consist of going to drive-thru restaurants or ordering pizza. By the time I was a teenager, I had zero self-confidence and carried it into being an adult. Even after I discovered the gym at eighteen and the underlying genetics given to me by my wrestler/bodybuilder dad, I still saw myself as that chubby kid with a pimply face that my mom would always point out.

It's easy to blame people from the past, and especially our parents, for the issues we have today, and that's very often the legitimate cause of many of those current issues—I mean, look at what you just read. But once we find where they originated, we have to do the work to fix them. So, for me, yes, my mom buried incredibly deep insecurities within me because of the constant letdown that accompanied empty promise after empty promise and always saying that I was fat. But it became my responsibility to take what I was dealing with when I was twenty-five—and by the way, this is still something I work through today at thirty-six—and find a way to remedy it. This is where my therapist, Joan, came in.

The exercise she suggested was to imagine standing in a room, and in that room with me was little me. So adult me is there, and I'm looking down at little kid me—scared, insecure little kid me. Joan said to go over to him and tell him that he's loved and to hold him. She encouraged me to practice this daily to begin the healing of the broken little me that was affecting the big, grown-up, insecure me. It did help, but I can say now, more than ten years later, as I look at Kai, I see so much of myself in him that it's as if this mental exercise has come fully to life. It's kind of strange, but in caring for him, it feels almost as if it's an extension of caring for myself.

I know the impact I'm having on him when I'm holding him and kissing him and telling him how much he's loved, because I know first-hand what not having these things does to a person—especially not having these things from a father. As I said above in the intro, *beautiful healing awaits you in this process.* By loving Kai as fully as I possibly can, it's shown me how to love myself more fully and my need for that love. If you don't think it's important to love yourself, simply . . . you're wrong.

The healing that awaits you is this—in loving him and laying his foundation in love and security, and building strength within him, you see that it's possible to have these things. Why is it possible? Because your son has them. Just because someone wasn't there to lay that foundation in you and your reality for so long was a painful, broken, and insecure one, you're showing yourself that a new reality can and does in fact exist because it's the reality that you're now creating. So the foundation that you're laying with your son is a foundation in him, but it's also a foundation in you. His advantage is that he didn't need to be broken completely to find the reality of such a foundation. His advantage is that you've been able to give him something you never had as a child. His advantage is having you as a father. And your advantage, now, is having him as a son.

THE SCIENCE

A lot of what I'm describing here is known as *attachment theory*. It has good and bad reviews just like anything, but when you investigate the literature, the science is overwhelmingly clear: the consequences for the closeness and bonding that happens in this practice are that neural connections develop in your child that lean more heavily to the side of security rather than insecurity.[2]

"At each developmental point, the infant
must have a close attachment with a
consistent caregiver to ensure protection
in the face of both internal changes
and environmental stimuli. Attachment
is, quite simply, a key to survival."[2]

Again, much of the brain's development, 90 percent, occurs very early on; from late pregnancy through the second year.[5] The development of the right brain is what's primarily taking place during this time, which is connected to the autonomic nervous system. This also brings forth the development of the limbic system—parts of the brain, including the amygdala and hippocampus, that participate in generating human emotion. These systems involve the function of stress response and coping capacities.

An important point here is that attachment facilitates an expansion of coping capacities—meaning, the more love you put on your son, the more he's able to handle stressful and painful experiences.[3,4] More presence, more warmth, more hugs, and more kisses program their brain to build more structures of security rather than insecurity.

Oxytocin is a neuropeptide that's released naturally by the body during these physical interactions. Oxytocin acts on eliminating stress-inducing hormones, improves overall mood, increases tolerance for pain, and finally can speed the process of healing. The absence of oxytocin yields increased levels of stress hormones, increased blood pressure, anxiety disorders, and rising fears.[9]

These are the biological changes and effects taking place in your little one, but there are also similar biological reconfigurations happening within you.

"Since dopamine neurons are sensitive to reward stemming from social interaction and can link reward to attachment experiences, they ground reward in cycles of caregiving actions."[6]

Physiological synchrony is the mechanism by which biochemical changes occur within the parent and child during interaction—it's a "close match of physiological states between parent-child dyads."[7] Following synchronous interactions, there's a release of dopamine and oxytocin within both the parent and the child.[6] The release of these neurochemicals further strengthens the bond between them and is a continuous feedback loop encouraging this attachment behavior.[8] Dopamine works in a cyclic way in motivating, rewarding, and reinforcing. It also plays a role in memory, mood, sleep, learning, concentration, and body movements.[10,11]

It seems that based on this, we're evolutionarily and biologically designed to establish and maintain attachment practices with our sons. There's healing happening here where your presence and love and caring as a father is now closing the loop on your potentially painful past. It's ending a generational rhythm that has no place in your boy's life—or your own. You're seeing things become possible that you thought to be impossible until this point. Your son knows the joy of healing without the burden of being hurt.

2

THE WRESTLER

When it was finally revealed to me by my cousin, Vicky, that my father was likely the 1980s WWF wrestler my mom was hanging around, a new journey started—a journey to talk with my real dad or at least figure out who he was.

Having spent a lot of my life without a dad, it was something I had gotten used to. In fact, it became something that I didn't think much about when I became an adult. If Mark hadn't reached out and connected with me when I was twenty-two, I'd have likely continued on in life giving an ever-decreasing amount of thought to who my dad actually was. But after I met Mark and found out he wasn't my biological father, I was interested in finding out more about the man that I was biologically linked to. Mark had said he remembered briefly meeting the wrestler in the '80s through my mom after I was born.

While we're here, let's not beat around the bush. From my perspective and much of what's been told to me, my mom was kind of a player. She was a wrestling groupie. She had blinding blonde hair and always the right amount of mascara, and was strikingly beautiful. Vicky was younger than my mom by about nine years and got to meet some of the wrestling greats from that golden era, like Jimmy "Superfly" Snuka, Andre the Giant, Tito Santana, Rocky Johnson, and a ton of others. In fact, when we did reach out to my biological dad, he said we got the wrong person and that it was Snuka we should be looking for.

It was Mark that made the initial contact with the wrestler in 2011. "I don't think this is going to go how you'd like it to," was what Mark said to me after having a call with him. Mark had reached out on my behalf, without my knowing, thinking that it would make for a smoother experience. He had already met Jim, the wrestler, many years before and would ensure Jim that I wasn't some lunatic looking for anything more than a chat over coffee. Jim was angry, and he threatened to call the police if we made any further attempts to contact him. He wasn't interested in exploring this any further than screaming at Mark over the phone.

A point that Mark tried conveying was the striking similarities that Jim and I shared. He had chased a wrestling dream, and I had chased a rockstar dream. Then he went to college and became a high school math teacher, and I went back to college but became a college math instructor. Then Jim retired as a high school principal—I also worked in administration but again at the college level. These were all things I had done before I knew about Jim. Genetics are crazy as hell.

It looked like we were at a dead end in this pursuit, and that was mostly correct until several years later, when I was thirty-five, and my wife bought me an ancestry kit for Christmas—I was twenty-five when Mark first reached out to Jim. The reason Erin, my wife, bought me the ancestry kit was because our son was on the way and we needed to know about family medical history and if there were any issues we should worry about.

"You look just like your dad."

After taking the ancestry test, it showed a close relationship to a man named Eric—likely an uncle. I looked at his picture posted on the ancestry website and saw a smile that looked like mine. I sent him a message explaining that there were several paths in the past that led me to believe Jim was my dad, and I assured Eric that I wasn't looking for anything, not even confirmation about this, but only family medical history. I'd mentioned Jim because there was a picture of them together on Eric's profile. Given the response from my biological dad several years prior, I didn't have high hopes.

The message, however, was received and responded to in kindness. Eric told me that the only thing the family dealt with was high blood pressure, and then he told me that I look just like Jim, his brother. My dad.

It was official. No longer just looking at old '80s wrestling clips on YouTube, but DNA testing, showed that the wrestler was indeed my dad.

I asked Eric recently what was going through his head when he got that message on the ancestry website back in March of 2020—he's passionate about building out his family tree and has been doing ancestry research for years. This is what he sent me:

> When you contacted me, my first reaction was, "Here's another relative who wants to find out how we are related." I usually check out my newfound relative's profile, and we

share a list of surnames. After this brief encounter, we wish each other good luck in our shared genealogy pursuit and part ways. Your contact, however, was different. First of all, you had an affiliation with my alma mater, Carnegie Mellon University, you lived in Pittsburgh, and most important, your resemblance to our family was uncanny. When you mentioned my brother, it was a huge shock. Initially, I wasn't sure how to react. I had heard rumors, but that's all they were. Now, these rumors were confirmed. Regardless of how Jim has reacted, I have the same reaction as my mother would have had . . . you are part of this family, and we love you and your beautiful family. I added you and your family to the family tree. You are my nephew, plain and simple. As the Navajos once told me, 'When you have your health and the love of your family, you are a very wealthy person.' Our lives are enriched knowing that you and your family are part of our family.

I may not have found a loving dad in this endeavor who wanted to sit down and talk about life over coffee or the many similarities that we share, but I did find a loving family that cleared much of the confusion and questions I had. Thank you for that, Uncle Eric.

I also found out that I have a sister, Donna, who was eighteen when I was born. I was raised as an only child, so this came as a welcome surprise. Donna has energy—good and beautiful energy. And a lot of it. I love her like I have known her forever. We look almost identical even though there are almost twenty years between us. I asked her as well what she thought when we first connected. She'd said that she was initially hurt and worried that her dad had cheated on her mom, but once we met and she found out how old I was, it was clear that Jim and Donna's mom had already been divorced by the time I was born. She said, "It hurt me to find out, once I met you and I loved you, that you lived your whole life without being loved by a dad, and that breaks my heart."

Even though Jim's family embraced me, he has not. Recently he agreed to answer some questions I had, but only through my sister, Donna. Their relationship is mostly estranged, with minimal contact between the two. When I sent the questions over, however, he changed his mind. I also sent him a picture of his grandson, Kai. His response to Donna was, "I don't want to ruin my life over something that happened more than thirty years ago."

It's unfortunate and sad that this was his response, and I'd be lying if I said it didn't hurt. Though, with all the pain and brokenness that life has shown me, I've learned that life isn't *all* pain and brokenness. Freedom can be found in forgiveness, and the flaws of others can teach you how not to be. *A good man learns from his mistakes. A wise man learns from the mistakes of others.*

This is the message I sent to Jim:

> First, thank you for doing this. Since the start
> of learning about you, I've never wanted any-
> thing, and I definitely never wanted to bring
> any strife to your family. I have to admit that
> it was pretty cool to see those videos of you

wrestling because I was such a huge fan of wrestling growing up. Actually, I was obsessed with it, so it was kind of amazing to find that I had it in my blood to love the sport. I hope learning about me hasn't brought you any anguish—I'm pretty normal, and I've had a lot of success in higher education. The reason I'm writing this book is to tell my story while also tying in biological concepts in the hopes of inspiring more men to be more present and more loving toward their sons.

If you can answer some of these questions, I'd appreciate it. If not, I understand. Thank you again for being part of this.

One last thing, as I'm sure you've been told, you have an absolutely beautiful, bright, and loving grandson named Kai. He's not only the light of my life, but he brings joy and light to everyone he meets—at only twenty-one months old. I do hope maybe someday you two will get a chance to meet. He also loves when I do wrestling moves on him like powerbombs and choke slams—as I said, wrestling is in our blood.

1. Do you remember my mom? Can you share anything about her that you might remember?
2. Did you have any idea at all about me?

3. If you did know about me, did you attempt to be in my life?
4. Do you consider my being born a mistake?
5. Would you ever consider meeting me for a coffee?
6. Do you know that I don't hold any ill will or animosity toward you?
7. Not only the wrestling thing, but did you know that I taught math and worked as an administrator at the college level? We have a lot in common for never having met. Not really a question, but do you have any comment about that?
8. Is there anything you'd like to say to me?

I guess he answered the last question, which would essentially void the others. His answer was no. And that's OK. If you happen to be reading this, Jim, it's OK. I forgive you. Even if you're not asking for forgiveness or think that you need it, I forgive you.

When I found out that I was going to be a dad, I was terrified and worried that I would have no idea how to do it. I'd never seen it before, and this whole twisting tale that you just read about left me without almost anything of a reference point as to what it meant to be a dad and to love a son. I mean, especially a son, because I hate sports, remember.

But through all of this and the moment Kai was in my arms at the hospital the day he was born, I learned something so simple and so profound—I didn't need to have had the experience of being loved the way that I now love him. Just because you weren't loved a certain way doesn't mean you can't love a certain way. You're not disqualified from loving because you weren't loved. More specifically, you're not disqualified from loving as a father because you didn't have a loving father. The love you'll find is as immediate as a flash of lightning and as easy and natural as breathing. There's really nothing that you need to learn—it's just there. It's there for you to give to him.

THE SCIENCE

Obviously, my dad wasn't there to instill in me the values he held regarding education and learning. But even without him around, I still managed to find a path that led me to pursuits similar to his. That's the power of genetic predisposition.

> **"Geneticists have always held true
> that the expression of a genetic trait
> in the phenotype is highly variable,
> largely depending on the environment
> to which the individual carrying the
> trait of concern is subjected."**[15]

Something maybe even more powerful is what's known as *epigenetics*. The word *epi* is from Greek, and it means "above."[17] Epigenetics suggests that environmental factors will influence the expression of certain genes that may have remained dormant otherwise. The *expression* of a gene simply means that it's turned on. The gene holds the code, or instructions, for how the biological organism will function and behave.[16] When the gene is expressed, this function or behavior will also be expressed outwardly in the organism.[12] By the actions we take and the things we do or do not do as fathers, this is establishing very real neural structures within our sons' brains that are being expressed because of the genes that are being expressed. Our love has an effect, absolutely, on a molecular level of development.

> **"We suggest that childhood adversity leads to persistent alterations in transcriptional control of stress-responsive pathways, which—when chronically or repeatedly activated—might predispose individuals to stress-related psychopathology."[13]**

That is a really scientifically confusing way of saying, being treated poorly in childhood can increase the chances of mental health problems, like major depression and anxiety disorders, as those children age. The part about "transcriptional control" is referring to what's going on at the molecular level, or the level of the gene. The genetic instructions, that I mentioned above, are carried out partially by this transcription process.[12]

The above quote comes from a study that examined gene expression in a group of sixty adults, half of which identified as having experienced childhood trauma while the other half did not. The group that did not experience childhood trauma was used as the control group in the study. It was found that after exposing the sixty participants to a stress test (the study referred to it as a "laboratory stress protocol") there were in fact changes seen at the molecular level. What they did to induce each fifteen-minute interval of stress was to do a mock interview and ask a math question that the participant had to solve mentally.

What they found was that there were a significant number of genes differentially expressed between both groups at 45-minutes and 180-minutes following the stress protocols. At 45-minutes there were 404 differentially expressed genes between both groups, and at 180-minutes there were 608 differentially expressed genes between both groups.[13]

Differential gene expression just means that different genes are being expressed between two groups. Understanding differential gene expression can help in identifying the causes as well as preventive measures in biological healthy states versus biologically diseased states.[14]

Based on the study mentioned here, people who experienced childhood trauma were significantly more likely to undergo genetic differentiation when exposed to stressful situations. This means that stemming all the way back to not being loved enough, kissed enough, hugged enough, held enough, and having all of that replaced with neglect and various abuse would trigger a response in their bodies all the way down to the molecular level of a gene signaling that they're not safe. They're not secure. They're not OK. Their same evolutionary response mechanisms that have been in place since saber-toothed tigers walked the planet come fully alive in situations that show even the slightest levels of stress induction. For them, a math problem and the threat of being eaten alive by a saber-toothed tiger have the same genetically triggered responses.

The quote above says that continued trauma in childhood likely increases a person's chances of experiencing various stress-related psychopathologies. Those psychopathologies can include major depressive disorder, bipolar disorder, schizophrenia, paranoid personality disorder, and social anxiety disorder.[13, 18]

Just because these are things that you and I may be dealing with now because of our broken pasts, does not mean we're required to impart these same things to our sons. Remember, it's not only physical abuse that can bring about these problems, but also neglect.

Lose yourself in every moment you have with your little one—they're fast, they're fleeting. Find a way to bring your mind and your heart to the present moment that you're gifted with having. Kiss and hold that little boy. Kiss . . . and hold . . . that little boy. In doing that, you're conquering and destroying the shadows of your past that so desperately want to break into the present. Don't let them. The only way to defeat those hateful shadows of the past is to lose yourself in the loving present that you're creating for your son. For yourself. For your family.

3

THE BEST PERSON I'VE EVER KNOWN

Aunt Doe taught me that love can be as much of a presence in a home as brokenness can be. When you've seen a lot of darkness, you start to think that only darkness can exist. You start to think that dysfunction is the standard function of living.

Aunt Doe was my grandmother's sister on my mom's side. Her and my grandma loved me and saw me as nothing short of gold when I was little. My grandma was the other best person I've ever known. They also kissed and hugged me as relentlessly as I kiss and hug Kai. I never wanted to go back home when I was with them, and it's likely because of them—actually, it's entirely because of them—that I never fully succumbed to the deepest moments of depression that I experienced as a teenager. In fact, one of the last things that I said to my aunt Doe was that if it wasn't for her, I wouldn't still be here. That's what I said to her when she was fighting and losing a battle with cancer in a hospital bed when I was eighteen.

**"Such a lonely day, and it's mine, it's a day
that I'm glad I survived."
—System of a Down**

That lyric always struck me because it really becomes a matter of surviving those deepest and darkest moments of depression. Being with my mom was a nightmare. Being with my aunt Doe and grandma was being awake from that nightmare.

Depression found me when I was around twelve years old, maybe earlier, but that's the furthest back I can remember of the feeling that I felt when I'd get home every day from school. I remember going into the house alone—my mom was usually at work—and I'd go into my room and just stare out the window. I don't even know how long I'd sit there. I know it was long, at least an hour or more at times. I would just stare out into nothingness while depression gripped me. Our cable and phone were usually shut off, and my mom really didn't like me to go anywhere, so I was usually stuck in an empty house with the only thing that I think kept me sane during this shit time—music and my guitar.

I'd lose myself in Korn albums, Slayer, Arch Enemy, and I'd practice guitar until my fingers literally bled to emulate these musicians I'd grown to idolize. The lyrics and the intensity of the music helped to pull me out of that dark room and put me somewhere else. It wasn't long until I realized that music could be my escape from this life that I hated. It was my escape emotionally, but I knew it could also physically pull me out of that rundown neighborhood and broken reality that I faced every day. My first guitar was an Ibanez, and it was my aunt Doe that helped me roll my quarters and gave me the rest of the missing funds to buy it. This was a special moment because the guitarists in Korn played the same brand of guitars.

My aunt was also the funniest person I've ever known. She was so far from politically correct that she'd have a hard time fitting in with the overly sensitive social media cancel culture that we find ourselves in today. I remember she had a cousin that was a priest, and at every barbecue or family event, she was the only person to get him to swear. She just made people feel and embrace their "human" when they were with her. And she accepted everybody. I have a lot of love and support for the LGBTQ+ community, and I think it started with my aunt.

Her daughter, Vicky, the one who told me about my real dad, had two best friends in high school—Marybeth and Stephen. Marybeth was a gay white woman who was in a relationship with a black woman, and Stephen was a gay white guy. There wasn't a single person who would walk through my aunt's door and not only feel welcome but also laugh their ass off the whole time they were with her. She hosted backyard wrestling matches while my friends and I would put each other through tables. She made incredible food, every holiday was at her house, and she made me forget how depressed I was because I was always too busy laughing with her.

When I was fifteen, my mom moved to California, and I moved in with my aunt Doe. I couldn't have been happier about it. I hung my Korn poster in the basement, set my guitar amp up, and enjoyed finally being away from—and what felt like being awake from—the nightmare of living with my mom. I would go to my aunt all the time and hug and kiss her in the kitchen and tell her she had to live forever because I couldn't live without her. For three years, I lived with my aunt

Doe and enjoyed every minute of it. The laughter, the food, the holidays, the memories. Everything.

I used to sleep on a couch at her house, and even today I still prefer sleeping on couches. When I was eighteen, I got a bad case of tonsilitis. I didn't have health insurance or any money, but I did have Aunt Doe. She made me sleep in her bed while she took the couch, made me toast and tea, brought me medicine, and got me feeling human again. While she was taking care of me, though, she started to have stomach pains, and her appetite started decreasing. I remember coming home at night after being out with my friends, and I would look into her room just to make sure she was OK. While she was sleeping, I'd watch to make sure she was breathing. This was before these stomach issues even started. I was just so terrified to lose her. Terrified. She showed me so much joy and love, and I couldn't imagine a day without it. I couldn't imagine a day without her. I had to know every night that she was OK.

The stomach pains persisted, and her appetite continued to diminish. She finally saw a doctor, which she kept putting off, and my worst fear came to life—it was cancer. It was an aggressive cancer that had metastasized throughout her whole body. There wasn't much that could be done for her. She was only sixty-two.

During a visit to the hospital, a couple weeks before we lost her, she was still her jovial and lighthearted, joyous self. She looked fine. She didn't look at all like this disease was quickly taking her from us. I was in the room with some other family members when the doctor came in. She began introducing us, "This is my sister, Barbara, my daughter, Vicky, my son, Nick." She introduced others, and then when she got to me, she grabbed my hand and said, "And this is my baby,

Mark." I'll never forget that moment or how loving her eyes were when she looked at me and did that. My aunt made me feel truly valued, loved, and cared for. All the things I never felt with my mom.

Two weeks later, my grandma called me crying and said to get to the hospital, "Aunt Doe is dying." I don't remember how she looked when I got there. My aunt was always so strong and always had the answers to all my questions—even when I asked her what VD was when I was fourteen because I heard it in an Eminem song. She never held back. Again, I don't remember exactly how she looked in that hospital bed because she was so weak and frail and not at all the person I remember her to be, but I do remember what we talked about.

Her breathing was labored, and her gaze was fixed on the ceiling. She was sedated pretty heavily to negate the pain, and I grabbed her hand just as she had grabbed mine a couple weeks before. She slowly turned her eyes to me, and I said, "Thank you. If it wasn't for you, I wouldn't be here. You saved me." She smiled and said, "Markie, don't cry. I'm going dancing."

It wasn't very long until I watched her return her gaze to the same spot on the ceiling and take her last breath. It was the greatest loss I'd ever known, and writing about it even now, eighteen years later, fresh tears are falling down my face. I still miss her so much. And I'm still so thankful that she saved me from what depression was trying to do to me all those years ago. If not for her, so much wouldn't exist.

I think that my grandma's love for her sister was so strong, and her heart broke so much when she lost her, that she was only willing to hold on for a few more years. In fact, she was sixty-two—the same age as my aunt when she had passed away. At twenty, I found myself again standing in a similar spot next to my grandma's hospital bed as she took her last breaths.

My family had actually told me that my grandma wasn't the best mom to her daughter, my mom, as she was growing up. They told me that she had treated my mom poorly, and much of that trauma absolutely contributed to my mom becoming how she became. I never knew that person in my grandma. She had changed into the person that I did know, which was only loving. I do wish she had been that person for my mom when she was young, but she wasn't, and my mom continued that same trend with me when I was young.

See, our brokenness tends to go back much further than we can really imagine. My grandma was unmarried and had a daughter very young in the 1960s. From what I've heard, her mother, my grandma's mother, was unkind to my grandma, but very loving toward my mom. This would be like me being cruel to Kai but loving to his children. And by the way, my mom does adore Kai.

There are generational patterns, curses, and rhythms that must be broken. That can be broken. I know because I broke them with Kai. I think the most damaging thing my mom did when I was little was lying to me, getting me excited about things that she never planned on fulfilling. Even before Kai was born, I would show up when I said I was going to show up for people. With Kai, it's a no-brainer that I'm there for him every day. The promises I make are the promises I'll keep to the absolute best of my ability. If any do have to be broken, he'll know exactly why. And that's an explanation I don't plan on having to give him very often, if ever.

Let me also say that, yes, much of what my aunt Doe and grandma did contributed to pulling me from those depths of depression, but along with that has been therapy and 40 mg daily of citalopram—my favorite SSRI.

I'm thankful for the brokenness, and I'm thankful for the hope that I could find something more in life than what I had always known. I'm thankful for my aunt and my grandma loving me the way they did—it helped me experience much of the hope I found after living through such hopeless moments.

THE SCIENCE

I think it's because I lost my aunt to cancer that I chose to major in biology as an undergraduate in college. I got very interested in neuroscience and exactly what's going on in people who experience depression. And that number of people is likely a lot more than you probably think it is. The global population of people living with depression is estimated to be 322 million or 4.4 percent of the world's population. To go along with that, anxiety disorders affect more than 260 million people, or 3.6 percent of the world's population.[19] Even though that's a lot, and it is, I think the real numbers are actually greater than what's been captured.

So many cultures play down the realities of mental health disorders—not the least of these being the culture many of us find ourselves in as dads that tell us what it means to really be a man. Crying about being sad is second to none when it comes to this strange societal parameterization of being a man. Even disliking sports isn't as bad or as bitch as talking about your depression and emotions.

We need to flip that conversation on its head. It is certainly something that's talked about more now than it was in the past, but it still needs to find even more voice. Depression is also one of those words that gets thrown around a lot—I think we need a clearer understanding of what it can mean. The World Health Organization explains depression in the following way:

> During a depressive episode, the person experiences depressed mood (feeling sad, irritable, empty) or a loss of pleasure or interest in activities, for most of the day, nearly every day, for at least two weeks. Several other symptoms are also present, which may include poor concentration, feelings of excessive guilt or low self-worth, hopelessness about the future, thoughts about dying or suicide, disrupted sleep, changes in appetite or weight, and feeling especially tired or low in energy.[20]

Any of that sound like you? What does taking care of your depression and mental health have to do with being a good dad and kissing your son? Everything. Absolutely and unequivocally everything. Depression will tell you not to kiss your son because you just don't feel like it, and you'll listen because you're depressed. Depression will tell you everything I'm writing here is bullshit, and you'll listen because you're depressed.

I think if my mom had been treated for the mental health problems she was facing, I might not be writing this book—so the philosophical question then becomes, was it a bad thing that I went through those bad things to get here? No, I'm thankful for the things that made me who I am, but my son doesn't have to experience those same things to become who he's capable of becoming. I can help him find a healthier path to become his best and fullest self without the mess it took to get me there. The catch is, I can't help him find healthy paths if I'm not on one. You can't help your son find healthy paths if you're not on one. And they're not paths of *arriving* at your fullest self but *becoming* your fullest self, which is an ever-expanding experience of continued growth.

> **"Most worryingly, adolescents with major depressive disorder are up to thirty times more likely to commit suicide."**[21]

Depression can also be genetically heritable. If someone has a parent or sibling with major depression, they are potentially two to three times more at risk of developing depression themselves compared with an average person. If the parent or sibling has had depression more than once, or *recurrent* depression, and it started earlier in life, from childhood through their twenties, there can be a four to five times greater chance of heritability.[22]

Because adolescents are thirty times more likely to complete suicide, and depression is something that can be inherited as mentioned above, it becomes a matter of life and death for us as dads to ensure we're being as honest as possible with ourselves and finding exactly the help that we might need. Along with this, again, because depression is heritable, we need to be mindful and aware if we begin seeing depressive symptoms in our children. If I'm simply oblivious to or have chosen ignorance regarding the medicines and therapies available that save lives, then I'm not holding up my end of the deal of being a dad. In 2019, the CDC reported suicide as the second leading cause of death in people aged ten to thirty-four. [23] I was thirty-four when Kai was born.

*Before I go on, call this number if you're
at the point of thinking depression
is winning: 1-800-273-TALK (8255)
or go to SuicidePrevention.org*

I've been taking a medication called citalopram for years. It's an SSRI, or selective serotonin reuptake inhibitor. It functions exactly the way that it sounds—it's a medication that targets the biological mechanism responsible for regulating serotonin and slows it down. What I mean by a *mechanism regulating serotonin* is that there are nerve cells, called *neurons*, that communicate with one another. There is a small space from one neuron to the next called the *synapse*. It's in this space where chemicals called *neurotransmitters* travel from one neuron to the next neuron to deliver a specific message. Serotonin is one such neurotransmitter.[24]

There's a gene in this process called hSERT, that has the instructions for making something called a *serotonin transporter*—remember, genes hold the instructions for how biological forms and functions are to be carried out within an organism. The job of the serotonin transporter, created by that hSERT gene, is to take the excess serotonin that's in the synapse and recycle it back into the neuron that initially sent it out. You can say *recycle*, or you can say *reuptake*, because it takes the serotonin back in after it's been released.[24]

The job of the SSRI, then, is to slow this process down so that the serotonin can stay in the synapse long enough for the message to be delivered from one neuron to the next. It's believed that some people have that gene, hSERT, working a bit too fast. Because of this, the serotonin isn't left in the synapse long enough to effectively bind to the receptors of the second neuron. And without this successful binding to the receptors, there isn't successful communication between the neurons.[24] In my experience, the message seems to be one that says, "Don't kill yourself." This isn't a joke or making light of what's going on. This has been my sincere lived experience with depression.

I'd heard a couple of years ago that citalopram can increase blood pressure, so I decided to cut my dosage in half without doing any real research. Obviously, the idea was to lower my blood pressure—really, I just needed to eat less pizza. I only took half of a pill for five days, and by day five, I looked at Erin, my wife, and told her I sincerely felt like I wanted to kill myself. Now, I wasn't planning on committing suicide, but the overwhelming depression that found me, because I'm a dumbass and cut my own dosage in half without talking to my doctor, was enough to take me all the way back to that bedroom window that I'd helplessly stare out of so many years ago. That same day I took my full dose and never played that game again. I'd suggest you not play that game either.

As a side note, my blood pressure did come down, but it was by eating fresh fruit every morning and, of course, eating less pizza. Exercise helps too. But definitely don't cut your own meds in half like a dumbass.

In conclusion, a study from 2017 showed that SSRIs do not increase blood pressure.[25] I'm a dumbass.

4

DREAMS

After my aunt died, I realized it was only me now. I started managing a pizza shop and focusing on music like I never had before. I wanted to be onstage and playing shows. I wanted to travel and never see the broken home I'd left behind. My friends and I put together a band called In the Wake. Because I was the only one out of my friends that knew how to scream—a vocal technique in heavy metal—I put my guitar down and picked up the mic.

We practiced in my friend Dan's basement for hours every day, putting together songs, covering songs of our favorite bands, and talking about how cool that first show would be. It wasn't long until we got our first show, and after I sang the hour-and-a-half-long set basically staring off to the side and at the ground, never making eye contact with the crowd, I realized I wasn't exactly electrifying onstage—but I could scream for over an hour without exhausting my voice, so that had to count for something. We also only had three original songs at the time, and if you didn't know who the band Killswitch

Engage was before our show, you definitely did by the end, having featured ten of their songs in our set.

After more shows and writing more original songs, we started getting a pretty good feel for putting on a performance. I got a little more electrifying onstage—what a great word. I'm laughing at myself right now. Dads get it. Dwayne Johnson probably gets it, too, since he was the "most electrifying man in sports entertainment." Alright, no more wrestling references or bad dad jokes.

We got good at getting the crowd to go crazy, and what was even crazier was when people were singing the songs we had written. They screamed along with every line and didn't miss a beat. I mean, these were lyrics I wrote in Dan's basement about my shitty childhood and failed relationships, and now I was onstage and people were screaming them back to me. It was surreal. It was awesome.

We played a show at a small VFW in Ford City, Pennsylvania. It was the second time we had played there, and in the time between our first and our second show there, we had put out an EP and our fanbase started growing. Because of that, there was a lot of excitement the day of that second show. From the moment we started the set with the first song, I couldn't hear anything—only the explosion of the crowd, an explosion that never died down. They were so on fire and screaming so loud for so long with such ferocity, I couldn't hear the guitars, the bass, the drums, or even myself screaming into the microphone. I could only hear them, and it was one of the most memorable and greatest experiences I'd ever had— to this day, it's a top-five moment.

This right here was it. This was what I had dreamed about, and it was happening. And in 2008, after we'd been a band for a couple of years, we got an email saying that we were going to play the Pittsburgh date of Warped Tour and headline the Ernie Ball stage. We all had tears that day and couldn't believe it was happening.

When we arrived at the pavilion, the same pavilion where we had been coming to see bands we loved and admired for years, from Korn to Ozzy Osbourne, we couldn't believe we were there—especially when we got picked up in a golf cart that would take us through the VIP section to where we were going to set up. Tour bus after tour bus, the VIP lanyards hanging from the necks of those we admired, and us on a golf cart riding through it all. It was very much this day that showed me dreams are not nearly as far out of reach as we might think they are.

I'd never seen a bigger crowd in front of me than I had on that day. The show was outdoors, the sun was shining, and there was a sea of people with fists in the air, excitement in their eyes, and moshing in their hearts, going absolutely fucking insane for us. My dream had come true. I was standing in it.

To get everyone even more fired up, one of our friends jumped onstage at the end of our set and threw demo CDs into the crowd. The only issue was that he threw them with a bit too much vigor, causing some of them to whiz through the air like ninja stars aimed at unsuspecting metalheads' heads. Our merch booth was set up next to the stage, and after we played our set, and after the onslaught of ninja star CDs, there was a line of people waiting to meet us. We took picture after picture and, shockingly, were asked to sign the CDs and t-shirts people were buying. We'd just played the biggest show of our lives and were now signing autographs—even now, it barely seems like it was real. But it was.

The only other thing that made this day a little sweeter was that the girl who had broken up with me two weeks before was standing next to our merch booth while we were signing autographs. That felt good. And it really brought to life the quote by Frank Sinatra, "The best revenge is massive success."

Sometimes I forget that I had this huge dream, chased it, and then actually caught it. It wasn't long after the Warped Tour show that a rep from Roadrunner Records connected with us and distributed our music through iTunes. This was 2008, so getting music on iTunes then was a lot trickier than it is now—usually you had to have some type of label representation.

In the Wake never actually landed a record contract, and we didn't become millionaires. We did write and record some amazing music that I'm still proud of, played incredible shows, connected with so many people, and ultimately did what we set out to do—we wrote music and played shows and signed a few autographs along the way.

In 2010 we were set to play our final show with another band we admired, Scary Kids Scaring Kids. Oddly enough—or maybe serendipitously enough—at the time, it was their farewell tour. Now, Scary Kids did have a record deal, in fact, they were signed with Immortal Records, which was the same label that Korn had been signed to for a while. Scary Kids also toured all over the world and were really at that next level that we hadn't quite gotten to. So of course, when I met them backstage and started talking to their keyboardist, I asked what the deal was—why were they walking away from this. His answer floored me. "I want to go back to school, man."

The reason his answer was so profound for me at the time and came at just the right time was that I had recently gone back to school myself and was incredibly conflicted with whether or not to give up the band that I had poured so much into for so long. Every day leading up to our last show, I was questioning it—who was I if I wasn't the lead singer for In the Wake? His answer was confirmation for me that I was on the right road. If he could give up his band that had done world tours, I'd be able to give up mine. That's not to downplay what we did as a band, but it was what I needed to hear.

That first year of college woke up some new things in me that weren't there before. I'd never realized how much I loved learning until I took those first few classes at that community college—the same community college that I would one day go back to teach at.

I found new passions and dreams in my heart, but this time they were related to school? This was odd because I fucking hated school. Well, high school at least. I barely graduated and failed geometry three times—yep, failed math three times and then ended up teaching math at the college level. Anyway, with my previous record of less-than-stellar academic performance or interest, this was jarring. The timing of going back to school and uncovering this new passion was perfect though regarding where we were as a band.

It seemed that we had taken In the Wake as far as it could go on our own, and the next phase was to find a label to sign us. Another local band in Pittsburgh, and friends we'd shared the stage with many times and one of my favorite bands, The Dream Intended, had gone to New York City to record with a real producer. This producer worked with real record companies and had deals with shows on MTV that played the music he produced.

I loved the recording they came back with and decided to reach out to the same producer they'd worked with through MySpace. Yeah, MySpace. That's where music was happening most in 2008. And to my shock, he responded. But he didn't respond saying to just go the normal route to book studio time and work with whoever was available. No, he was so in love with our sound that he wanted to record the whole album himself. He immediately started setting plans in place to record the album, hold a record release party in New York, and connect us with a booking agent that would set up a touring schedule. I couldn't believe this was happening. I mean, this was *really* it! We were really about to fucking make it and blow up! There was only one issue—an issue that would cost us the opportunity.

Eight thousand dollars.

That was the cost to record the album, and for a couple members of the band, it wasn't worth it. I was deflated and defeated, and following argument after argument, push after push, I remained defeated. We never went to New York, we never recorded a full-length album, we never had the record release party, and we never toured the album that never was. My heart was broken watching our potentially explosive dream wither into nothing. But was it all for nothing? Absolutely not.

It was our last show that I saw the impact we'd made as a band, especially when so many people came up to me with tears in their eyes saying how much our music meant to them. A good friend who was a local promoter, had helped get us on many of the bigger shows we had played, and had worked with hundreds of bands told me that with In the Wake going away, he felt like he was losing a piece of himself. He said In the Wake wasn't just some other local Pittsburgh metal band, but what we did mattered. He explained that we got to experience a lot of success and accomplishment that we should be proud of. It meant a lot because I know this guy didn't just say these kinds of things to anyone. Another friend said that after I told her we were playing our last show, she listened to our CD nonstop, and when I closed the show that night thanking everyone for coming out, she was a ball of tears.

"We won't allow our dreams remain unseen."
—In the Wake

And we didn't. We did not allow our dreams to remain unseen. We played our hearts out and had the time of our fucking lives doing it with people we loved. I can honestly look back at this with a full heart and no mention or thought of the words, *what if*. . .

What if **I put a band together and chased**
this thing with everything in me?

I did.

What if **I played every show with my**
whole heart and left it on the stage?

I did. After that first show, at least.

What if **I believed unbelievable**
things could happen?

I did, and I watched them happen.

What if is something that I never want to experience in life. *What if* is something I never want my son to experience in his life. It would be really hard for me to tell him how sweet and incredible a dream can be if I never tasted them myself. Usually when you tell someone that something tastes good, they ask what it tastes like. That's a hard question to answer if you didn't actually taste it.

If you're wondering, dreams taste like chicken. I'm kidding—they taste like purpose.

In 2014, the lead singer of Scary Kids Scaring Kids passed away. Tyson and I shared the exact same birthday, even down to the year. He was only twenty-nine. The memory of having had the opportunity to play alongside him and his band will be one I'm forever grateful for. The night we played that show with them, I learned two things: First, dreams are possible, in fact, likely. Second, dreams can change, and it's OK when they do. Thanks for taking us for a ride that night and putting on a hell of a show. Rest easy, Tyson.

THE SCIENCE

There are biological mechanisms underlying the pursuit of a goal and goal attainment. It's important for you to know the goals and dreams you have, and it's equally important to go after them. As I mentioned above, they're closer and more likely to happen than you think they are. Going after the thing or things that set your heart on fire has everything to do with being a dad that loves his son, and that's because you're able to love more fully.

When you live your life outside of and away from that what-if zone, your heart finds fullness because you're doing more to walk in your life's purpose. You're spending and have spent enough time with yourself to know the things that reside within you that want and need to be expressed in your actual lived experience. Living this way, living fulfilled, breaks your heart wide open, but in a good way, so that you can share everything that's within it with those you love.

When you're walking through every day disgruntled, aggravated, agitated, stressed, depressed, and resigned from living, it's really hard for you to be the opposite of those things for the people you want to be the opposite of those things for. When you're full, you'll bring fullness. When you're at peace, you'll bring peace. When you're hopeful, you'll bring hope. And when you're walking in love, that's just the thing that you'll bring to your relationships.

When the brain is stimulated by achievement, it releases dopamine, and dopamine acts as a motivator.[26] In chapter one, I explained that dopamine has a role in sleep, mood, and other physiological experiences that lend to our overall health. The release of dopamine means that our bodies are naturally set up to reward us when we seek a goal and pursue it.

There's also research that suggests individuals will adjust their hope in response to the success and failure of pursuing goals. There is a reciprocal influence between hope and goal accomplishment. Hope leads to goal pursuit, and it is adjusted based on the goal's level of success. When good progress is made on a goal, hope cognition is reinforced, and when good progress isn't made, hope diminishes.[27] This is a reason to remember the things we've accomplished as we continue forward in accomplishing new things. Remember your wins.

You've had more than you're giving yourself credit for, and that will help you push forward to achieve more and grow more.

I've also found that there may be nothing more rewarding than seeing our children succeed. I'm fairly early in this process, but when Kai was seven months old, he advanced in his swim class to the next level that's typically reserved for two-year-olds. In that moment I knew all about fatherly pride and joy. I was calling relatives, posting pictures on Facebook, and jumping around like a madman when my wife came home and told me about it.

We talked about this already, but there is a significant level of responsibility that I have as his dad in the development of his brain early on. And I want to do everything I can to ensure that his brain's functioning is optimal. To whatever extent I can lend to ensuring this, I'll do it. That natural release of dopamine and other helpful neurotransmitters in him is, in part, one of my responsibilities. I can see that responsibility through by implementing the attachment practices described earlier, the practices that form his brain during those crucial developmental periods early in his life. As he gets bigger, I want Kai to have a healthy relationship with understanding goals and attaining them. His understanding starts with what he sees, and he's looking at me a lot. Your son is looking at you a lot. For them to understand goals and achieve a life they want, which is what we desire most for our children, we have to be doing the same thing with our own lives—the lives that they're watching and a part of every single day.

What will get you closest to your goal is to first know what it is, write it down, imagine and feel the achievement emotionally prior to actually obtaining the goal, and lose yourself every day in working toward it. When you narrow your focus to the thing you want to achieve, there's a group of cells at the base of the brain that brings to your attention the things you've deemed necessary and relative to your dream. This is called the *reticular activating system* (RAS). The RAS filters in things from your day-to-day experience that relate most to the goal you're working toward. You'll pick up things you didn't notice before and be able to seamlessly incorporate them into your achievement strategy.[28, 29]

Studies in neurology have shown that the brain cannot distinguish between reality and imagined reality. When we create in ourselves a state by envisioning our dream's attainment, the brain works to maintain that state and bring about that state as often as it can. Because this state releases dopamine, the brain wants to bring you back to it as often as it can. This is where activation of the RAS comes in. It works to create and maintain the state of our envisioned goal's achievement and success. It's working to introduce your imagined reality to your lived reality. That's because it can't distinguish between the two. It just wants all of the realities, imagined and lived, to be met with the same state that's brought on by achievement.[28, 29]

A quick example in my own experience is that since I started writing this book, I have noticed more dads with their children, and more specifically their sons. I see more interactions around me of loving relationships between fathers and their children, and it feeds my inspiration and the fire to keep writing this. It feeds my hope that there are loving relationships between fathers and sons. It does exist and can exist for more fathers and sons. I want to see lives changing because sons are being loved because dads are learning how to and allowing themselves to fully love their little ones. My RAS is firing because this is something linked to my goals and something I've regarded as extremely important.

I can see more boys growing into strong men because the strong men in their lives kissed them, held them, hugged them, and loved them. And I'm seeing that kissing, holding, and hugging more and more around me every day.

Along with this, I know that working toward my goals and taking daily action on them has made me a more present and loving father to my son. Because I take the time every day to work on things that I know are linked with my dreams, when I'm with Kai, I'm nowhere else. He has my full attention, my full being, and I'm able to mindfully experience every moment I have with him—every moment that, as I look back and think about it, seems like a flash of lightning. It feels like Kai was born this morning, but he's already almost two years old.

I'm thankful that I practice something that would seem counterintuitive—why spend any amount of time away from him, especially if it's time doing something some might deem as "optional" when I could just be with him instead of in a café writing? Because the time spent with him after doing this work will hold so much more value. It's because I find fulfillment in the work I'm doing, that I can bring fulfillment to our relationship. I bring all of me and not a distracted me that's thinking of what I could have done or should have done or could be doing or should be doing. I am doing exactly what I should be doing because I did what I needed to do before I got to him. The quality of the time we spend together is magnified because I took time to work on the dreams I have and goals I've set that go along with those dreams. I'm a better dad because I show up for myself just as I show up for him.

I told you before, if you don't think loving yourself is important, you're wrong.

5

THE VILLAGE

I started hearing this expression a lot when I became a dad—"It takes a village." The African proverb, "It takes a village to raise a child," suggests it takes many people coming together for the good of the child. Kai has so many aunts and uncles that don't have even a drop of blood in common with him, including his uncle Arge—one of my best friends that was the drummer for In the Wake and is also Kai's godfather. Uncle Arge also coproduced the song I wrote under my Idol Killers moniker, "Kai's Song." The Idol Killers is a music project I started in 2020 when we were all in COVID lockdown. Without an open Starbucks in sight, I started playing around with Garage Band at my dining room table and soon had about four songs that I released independently. It's easier to get music out now than it was in 2008.

Once our last show was behind us and I was fully invested in completing a degree, the road definitely did not get easier. I was a full-time student and working three nights a week delivering pizza. After In the Wake dissolved, I found myself in the precarious position of learning that Mark wasn't my real dad and had to find a new place to live.

Dan's parents, those saints that let their son's metal band practice in their basement and rumble their entire house for years, were always like second parents to me and immediately opened their doors when I needed a place to stay. This wasn't the first time I had lived with them, and it wouldn't be the last.

My life was somewhat unraveling in 2010—In the Wake was no more; I didn't have a dad again; my girlfriend, not the one from Warped Tour, broke up with me; I was asked to leave the worship band I started at a church because that ex-girlfriend was also in the band (though, I might have threatened to beat the shit out of any guy she might bring to church, so I get that one); and finally, I was in my third year of college and failing.

Things were really going great.

It was around this time, while life was beating the ever-loving shit out of me, that I asked God what he thought I was made of. I remember being in the shower and just kind of shaking my head. I was thinking of everything that was piling up and saying out loud, "Man, you just do not know what I'm made of . . . I really can't take on much more . . . There's no way you can know what I'm made of. This is way too damn much!"

I got out of the shower, walked into my room, and *very* reluctantly picked up my Bible—yes, I read the Bible and have a relationship with God and still swear and am still "human." That's the point of the relationship.

One of the cool things about God is his sense of humor. I opened "randomly" to Psalm 103:14, which says, "For He knows what we are made of, remembering we are dust."

Get the hell outta here.

I just said over and over how much you don't know what I'm made of for your response to be, "I know what you're made of." That still blows my mind even today.

I lived with Dan's parents until I found a very small apartment not far from the university I was attending. The studio apartment was actually an attic, and even though they called it a studio apartment, it was an attic. In fact, it was so hot and so attic that I had to take NyQuil just to fall asleep because I couldn't afford air conditioners for the windows the first summer I was there.

I stayed committed to school and inevitably finished. Throughout the experience of being an extremely broke college student, I had a lot of people, from academic counselors to cafeteria workers, who were more support to me than I can ever thank them for. These people had no reason to come alongside me to help and support me in ways that went beyond their roles in the colleges—like giving me free food or paying my $20 graduation fee from the community college or talking me into becoming a math tutor, which would ultimately lead me to a successful career in higher education.

Obviously, my aunt and my grandma were part of my village growing up, but after I lost them, more people seemed to step in and kind of love me for no reason. I'm glad I never let some type of pride stand in my way of letting other people help me—especially when the person who came alongside to help me when I was broke and living in that attic was, of all people, my mom.

"How ridiculous and how strange to be surprised at anything which happens in life."
—Marcus Aurelius

She was truly the last person I ever expected help from, but she was there. It's easy to paint someone as the villain, and she was the villain, I assure you, but when they actually show up for you, it really fucks with the storyline—life will often fuck with the storyline. She sent me the $400 rent every month until I finished school. She valued education, and this was her investment in me.

Pride or anger or unforgiveness could have stepped in and refused any kind of help from her. I mean, this was the person who gave me that first memory of seeing her cut her wrists with a damn steak knife, the person that fed me empty promise after empty promise, burying every insecurity imaginable into the fabric of my being, the person who moved to California when I was fifteen—and even though I was happy to see her go, looking back on it now, it does kind of feel like abandonment, and I guess that's because it was.

She was the person who lied about even being my mom to her friends and coworkers, the person that I could never have a conversation with without my blood immediately boiling. She was the person I hated, but she offered me help when I needed it the most. And I accepted the help. She was the person who took an iron to my face, stopping just short of one hell of a scar—who I fucking hated—and she offered me the raft when I was drowning at sea. And I took her hand and accepted the help.

Maybe I felt like she owed it to me for the nightmarish upbringing. Or maybe I just realized that I needed help, and she was the person that showed up—as unbelievable as it was. We can't pick our saviors, I guess. We can decide if we do need some saving, though, and if we want to accept that saving.

You can't do life alone. You weren't meant to. Especially as a man and as a dad, there's a level of broken thinking that says you have to push through everything life throws at you alone, or you're not man enough. You're not strong enough if you need help. You're the hero of your story; no one can help you.

Strength isn't found in ignoring life's assistance. Strength isn't found in refusing help, even if the source of that help is one you wouldn't expect in a million lifetimes—or one that you wouldn't even necessarily want. Strength is found in not assisting life with making things more difficult than they already very much are. Believe me when I tell you that life does not need your help to make it harder. But you need help when life does get hard—which is often.

My mom and I have had a lot of conflict and trauma within our relationship, but I will always remember this time in my life when she stepped in to help me at a time when I really needed it. I'll always acknowledge and appreciate her for that. I'll also always acknowledge and appreciate her for introducing me to horror movies as a kid and forever putting the spirit of Halloween in my heart. I have the original Universal Studios Monsters tattooed on my leg, and when asked why I got it, my sincere answer is that it's the only thing my mom and I ever agreed on and enjoyed together.

The people who have made up my village, and continue to make up my village, go from family to friends and everyone in between. I agree with the poet John Donne, when he wrote, "No man is an island." We cannot do this life alone, and we weren't meant to.

Life is unbearable and crushing at times, so we have others who can help us bear the weight. Life is also beautiful and joyous at times, so we have others to celebrate with.

"Happiness is only real when shared."
—Christopher McCandless

Being a parent isn't easy, and it's not always filled with moments of pure euphoric bliss. You need help, and there are more people around you to help than you realize. Let them. Go a step further, men, and ask them.

THE SCIENCE

I'm so thankful that I had my aunt, my grandma, and my cousin Vicky as I was growing up. If not for them, I would have been totally alone in dealing with my mom and all the issues that were dictating her actions. Those issues did have an enormous impact on me, but the impact was lessened because of these other ladies.

I'm also thankful for Vicky seamlessly stepping into the role of being Kai's Nunnie. My mom and I still have a mostly contentious relationship, so I'm glad Kai gets to experience that grandmotherly love not only from Erin's side but mine as well. In fact, it was Vicky who immediately calmed me when I was in my freak-out phase of learning I was going to be a dad. Because of her joy and tears of excitement, I realized it was going to be OK. I wasn't in some kind of trouble.

It's this village experience that I've had that shows me how important it is. To have people come alongside of you and lift you up for no reason other than love is one of the better experiences we get to have in life. Because Kai already has so many people that love him outside of just me and Erin, as he gets older, he'll be better able to trust. Seeing that love can and often does come out of nowhere, he'll hold more of an expectation for love and trust in the relationships he builds.

Even though parents may be a child's primary caregivers, a family does not exist in a vacuum. Social connectedness has been defined as those subjective psychological bonds that people experience in relation to others, including, for example, a sense of belonging and feeling cared for . . . There is much evidence that strong, positive connections are linked to positive mental health and well-being, especially in times of stress or trauma.[30]

This explains that strong bonds are established by various social supports outside of the immediate familial context.[30] It also explains in that last part that there is a positive influence on mental health during turbulent times when a person can look outside of the immediate family where the stress is initiating and find reprieve in others. This reinforces my thought of thankfulness for having others around when my mom was losing her damn mind in front of me and on me.

The important thing to take away from this is an echo of what I mentioned earlier. You don't have to have had the direct love of a father to be capable of loving as a father should love. It's OK that the love and support you got came from outside relatives or friends. Don't discredit the love that was shown to you, even if it wasn't from the person you thought it should have come from.

Obviously, we think our moms should have loved us more than life, but sometimes that isn't the case, and it's a grandma or an aunt or a friend's mom that loves us in the way we need. Don't let that gift of love ever become shrouded or diminished because it isn't the love you thought it should have been from the person you thought should have been giving it to you.

And if there wasn't anyone there at all when you were growing up, there are people now that want to love you. Let them. Hell, I love you! I'm a support for every dad reading this book, trying to find his way to loving as infinitely as he's being called to love. Don't do this life alone. Don't fear the ask of those around you. Allow yourself to be loved both when you look back through your past and by those wanting to love you now.

Another critical component and extension of the benefits found with having a village are the positive biological effects of social connectedness.

> Data from Bennett et al. (2006) provide an interesting biological perspective on the role of connectedness. These researchers followed healthy older people who, on first contact, showed no signs of Alzheimer's disease pathology. Yet, at postmortem examination years later, they found greater evidence of tangle density (a marker of such disease) among those who were least socially connected.[31]

This shows that with more social interaction and social belonging, there are preventative health benefits yielded. A lot of men tend to feel that they need to go at life alone. And there are indeed a lot of things that must be done alone and without others—but not everything.

Again, the message within these pages is to get you to be the best father you can be for your son. Much of the focus, though, has to remain on you so that you can become better and, in this moment, the best version that you've ever been. Becoming the best version of yourself is ongoing. There isn't truly a destination with this but only continual growth. You're a better father today than you were yesterday because you've done more for yourself today than you did yesterday. And tomorrow the trend continues as you continue building yourself so that you can build your son.

Build yourself so that you can build your son.

Every day, *every day*, do things that bring out and build within you the things that are making you a great father.

Counter to social connectedness, social isolation can have damaging effects on biological pathways related to stress. There's a release of cortisol, cytokines, and other biochemical substances that put pressure on the immune system, which breaks down your resistance to illness.

The hypothalamic-pituitary-adrenal axis, which is a portion of the brain that we've talked about, is responsible for the body's response to stress both in the environment and within the body.[31]

> In the absence of factors, such as social support, to buffer against the stress response, there is slower adrenocortical recovery which, when cumulative, can accelerate physiological decline. Supportive networks are believed to buffer these effects, controlling the body's response to heightened arousal and stress (Uchino 2006) and, through this, providing protection against damaging neurodegenerative outcomes.[31]

When engaged in social connectedness rather than social isolation, our bodies' coping capacities increase, and we are less biologically vulnerable to illness.

"It has been argued and found that social
networks provide a basis to suppress
neuroendocrine responses, which reduces
vulnerability to disease development."[31]

Regarding people that have increased social connectedness and social support, it's been shown that there is a decrease in overall cortisol levels and an increase in overall serotonin levels. **Additionally, blood pressure is lowered** in people that have strong social support.[31] So again, don't cut your medication in half to lower your blood pressure like a dumb ass; just get some friends.

6

CALIFORNIA

In the intro, I talked about the Universe doing interesting things when we make our minds up about something. In Paulo Coelho's book, *The Alchemist*, he writes, "When you want something, all the universe conspires in helping you to achieve it."[12] It's such a massively important lesson for us to show our sons that they can bravely step out into their lives and chase their dreams. It sounds simple, and that's because it is. However, it's hard to explain something with never having had the experience of it—that's why this starts with you. You must be the one who has and continues to pursue the things your heart is telling you to do. These aren't empty words. This is creating the way for your son to see the unending possibilities within his own life when he looks at yours. This is a message that bears repeating—know the things in your heart and pursue them.

Once I graduated with my bachelor's degree, I started working full-time in the community college as a student success coach and a math instructor. I really loved the work I was doing. I found crazy fulfillment in working with students and teaching. Seeing people see themselves doing things they were initially unsure of because of their own self-doubt and succeeding in those things was something I knew I wanted to do forever.

I mean, I could practically feel people's blood pressures rise when I'd just mention the word "fraction." But after some life coaching—you have to be a life coach to teach math—many students saw that they were able to conquer the thing they had feared most. I often had the experience of seeing students start out in those prerequisite math courses filled with fear and anxiety, only to come back a few short years later as full-fledged nurses or graduates in other programs, brimming with pride and confidence and gratitude.

Zig Ziglar has a great line that says, "You will get all you want in life, if you help enough other people get what they want." Isn't it interesting that finding our own fulfillment often comes by way of helping others find theirs?

After some time working for the college, I felt something shifting in my heart. At the time, I was single and making more money than I ever had before, so I was traveling every chance I could out to Los Angeles. I loved flying out and exploring beach community after beach community, from Santa Monica down to Laguna. With every trip there, it started getting more and more difficult to go back to Pittsburgh. Inevitably, moving there became something I knew I needed to do.

The job at the college also started to feel like more of a burden than a blessing. Not the teaching or working with students, but the dean that I reported to started making things more difficult than they probably should have been for me to help the students. I guess it was partially because I had a good relationship with her boss, the president, and this seemed to spawn some resentful and snide actions within her toward me. She started making my life as miserable as possible.

The moment I realized I was waking up five days a week miserable and filled with dread was the moment I realized I needed to make a change. And a change I made.

I quit the fucking job and moved to California.

Yep, just like that. Change happens instantly rather than over time like we mistakenly think it does, especially regarding the changes we need to make in our lives. The moment our brain shifts and we make the decision for change, that's the moment when change instantaneously happens. Tony Robbins talks about this, and I find it to be absolute fact. My advice here is if you're miserable, fuck it, move to California.

I'm joking. California isn't necessarily the change or move you need to make. But you do probably need to say "fuck it" to one or a few things in your life. Chances are, you probably need to quit the fucking job, too, or some form of something in your life that's sucking the life out of you. Do things that bring life to your life, not take away from it. You can't bring life and love to any relationship you have unless you have light and love within yourself—and sometimes you get there by saying those two glorious and empowering words—*fuck it*.

As cheesy as this may sound, it holds truth: your dreams are waiting for you. A better, more joyous and fulfilled you is waiting for the not-so-joyous unfulfilled current you. If you want to live a life that you love and be as complete as you can be in raising your child, you have to do the things that are in your heart. It doesn't matter how hard or unrealistic they may seem. And it seems that way because your vantage point currently sucks. It's a vantage point of inaction and perceived security. The moment, and it is a moment, that you take that first terrified step out, you'll find strength and clarity. Your vantage changes just slightly enough that you see that it's possible. And truly, that's all you'll need.

Most people want to wait until they get all their ducks in a row before they make any significant change. But there's an interesting secret that I've discovered—there are no fucking ducks. You'll never have everything exactly as you think you should have it before you do the thing or things you want to do. Just remember, while you're looking at your dreams and the responsibilities you have, and while you weigh what to do, keep this shining truth close to your heart: There are no fucking ducks.

You know what needs to be changed. Change it.

I had an interesting dream right before I moved West. Like a while-I-was-sleeping kind of dream. I dreamt that Oprah called me and invited me to be on a show she was hosting with Tony Robbins. In the dream, when I got the call, I was standing next to a lighthouse during either the evening or early morning because it was dark out. We hung up the phone, and I woke up. The dream brought a lot of peace with it, and I decided even more fully to go to California when I woke up. I also realized that there were no lighthouses in Pittsburgh, so it seemed like a pretty clear sign.

I drafted the email and attached my resignation letter. I sat there a while in my office and read over it several times and then continued to sit there and think about it and read over it several more times. I was in a mostly good job with great benefits, I was just finishing my first year of graduate school, which was partially being paid for by the college I worked at, and I had absolutely nothing lined up. No job, not even a place to stay. Just a plan to sell everything I owned, except for clothes and books, and drive west. That was it. And it was terrifying.

I sat there with that very present fear and prayed. I asked God if this was really where I was being called. Was this *really* what I was supposed to do? Amidst the incursion of fear, I felt a peace in my heart that couldn't have been larger than the point of a needle. The smallest most infinitesimal presence of peace was in my heart, and it seemed to cut straight through the fear.

I sent the email.

I learned that when facing a decision, it's often the one that's most terrifying that we're likely being called to make because that's the one that will take the most faith. And why does it feel so much better to walk toward our dreams in faith? Let me explain what happened right after I sent that email.

As a reminder, not only did I not have a job lined up, but also I didn't have anywhere to live or even stay outside of my leased car. Oh yeah, the car was leased. So I would have to find a job pretty quickly if I wanted to keep the car. The $11,000 that I pulled out of my 401(k) would only last so long.

You pulled money out of your 401(k)?

Yeah. Had a dream. Went after it. Cashed that bad boy in to help get me there.

A few days after sending the email and cementing my decision, my friend Dan's parents called me—the ones that I'd lived with and that let our band practice in their basement. Apparently, they had a distant family member recently pass away, and the family was looking for someone to move into this person's condo and keep it up while it was being prepared to be sold. Since they knew I was leaving my job and didn't really have much going on at the time, they asked if I could stay there and keep the place up. It was in Los Angeles. For the first three months of living in California, I lived in a two-bedroom condo with a heated swimming pool and a jacuzzi rent-free.

> "When you really want something, the whole universe conspires in helping you to achieve it."
> —Paulo Coelho

I always think about this with a bit of mixed emotions. The family member that passed was distant and had little interaction with their family. In fact, it was their brother-in-law's brother, and those two really hadn't interacted much over the years. Obviously, you don't want someone to die so that you can fulfill your dream, but the family was truly in need of someone to be in that area to work with the realtor that was prepping the place to go on the market. And I was truly in need of a place to stay. It was a long process, and because I was there, the family had to make fewer trips west to ensure things were moving as they should. They were extremely thankful to me, but obviously my gratitude toward them for allowing me to stay in such a beautiful place for so long while I got my bearings is more than a simple "thank you" can hold. But nonetheless, thank you. Thank you so much for helping me.

When I got to California, I expected a job offer, a new apartment, and a call from Oprah. Within the first week, at least. Two weeks max. I thought success and Teslas would greet me the moment I crossed the state line into California. It didn't exactly go like that.

The time leading up to leaving Pittsburgh, I began my campaign of sending out as many applications as I possibly could to every college I could find in Los Angeles, from UCLA to USC.

After three months of being in California, twelve interviews, over seven hundred applications submitted (that's not a typo), and paying my bills with the last of the $11,000 (that went faster than I thought it would), I got an offer from USC.

It was at the absolute last possible moment. The condo had sold, I only had a few days to leave, and all my money was gone. It was the last possible moment determining whether I'd be able to stay in California or if I had to go back to Pittsburgh with my tail between my legs asking for my old job back. The call came through, and I accepted it. I found an apartment and was even making more money than I was when I was in Pittsburgh.

The night before I got the offer from USC, I had another interesting dream. You probably know the story from the Bible about Jesus stopping a crowd from stoning a woman, Mary Magdalene. I dreamt that I was standing between her and the crowd just before they were about to stone her. Then Jesus was there, pretty much out of nowhere, and talked to the crowd. As the story goes, they didn't throw any stones. After this, the dream kind of warped, and I was standing alone in a dark room. It was a big room that seemed to be connected to some kind of industrial plant. Suddenly, Jesus walked through the door, but he was wearing modern clothes. He looked like an average person—long hair and a jean jacket. He stood in the middle of the dark room facing away from me and put his head down and his arms up, and light shone from the ceiling down on him. I woke up. But I woke up to total peace. More than peace—total faith. I knew, somehow, I was going to get the job I'd interviewed for the day before. And I did, in fact, get it.

It's kind of hard to explain all these dreams I had—especially leading up to the California move and also while there in California. They were like strange encrypted messages that popped up along the way of chasing my real-life dreams and brought assurance with them.

I think once we connect with our hearts and understand where they're calling us to go and we actually start going, it opens us up to being more receptive to things we can't see. The Universe, or God, or a Higher Presence, communicates with us even more deeply and more openly than it did before we were walking in such faith. Faith seems to be the language of these energies, so I guess it makes sense that once we step out in faith, we start to speak and understand their language a bit more. We were always being deeply spoken to, but we just weren't positioning ourselves to perceive it.

I don't mean for this to sound too heady or overly spiritual. But I do think that when you and I fully embrace the yearnings of our hearts, we see things and feel things and experience things that others don't. And that's because we do things that others won't or aren't willing to do.

I woke up early one morning and stared out of my apartment window at the palm trees swaying in the distance. Drinking hot coffee, I took all of it in. The sun was just coming out, and the trees swayed lazily against the dark yet lightening cloudless blue sky. My dream was to live in Los Angeles, California. Here I was, living in Los Angeles, California. It had happened. I had made it. Behind the scenes, life was preparing to beat the shit out of me.

THE SCIENCE

We can all probably agree that if we're going to a job every day that we hate, it's causing us stress. For me, once I start dreading the next day or especially the next week—like when you haven't even left the office on Friday, and you're already pissed off about Monday—that's when it's time for a change. The moment I start referring to Friday as "Fri-YAY," it's time to move on.

> Any intrinsic or extrinsic stimulus that evokes a biological response is known as stress. The compensatory responses to these stresses are known as stress responses. Based on the type, timing and severity of the applied stimulus, stress can exert various actions on the body ranging from alterations in homeostasis to life-threatening effects and death. In many cases, the pathophysiological complications of disease arise from stress and the subjects exposed to stress, e.g., those that **work** or live in stressful environments, have a higher likelihood of many disorders. Stress can be either a triggering or aggravating factor for many diseases and pathological conditions.[33]

What all this is saying is that working a job you hate can kill you. Or at the very least make you more susceptible to colds. Either way, why take the chance?

> **"In experimental studies, stress leads to morphological remodeling as well as molecular, neurochemical and electrophysiological changes that, it has been suggested, mediate the cognitive deficits observed in depression, anxiety and other mood disorders."[34]**

Stress has physical effects and alters various structures within the anatomy of the brain. The quote above is saying that stress will produce and mirror similar mental health issues as those seen in people suffering from depression, anxiety, and other mood disorders. This happens by way of the physical alterations brought on by stress occurring all the way down to the molecular level.

> **"Stress influences the structure and function of the amygdala and clinical investigations have shown that neuroanatomical changes in the amygdala precede those that are observed in the hippocampus of patients with mood disorders, in particular depressive illness patients."[34]**

This shows, further, that the physical alterations that stress produces are congruent with the alterations seen within patients with mood disorders, specifically those with depression. Stress can literally physically reconfigure your brain structure, bringing about illnesses such as major depression.

Experiencing high levels of stress also influences memory. Stress yields an increase in plasma concentrations of glucocorticosteroids, which, over an extended time, can lead to atrophy of the hippocampus. Because the hippocampus is directly connected to memory function, memory is adversely affected in high-stress environments.[33]

Patients with what's known as Cushing's disease, a disorder involving the excessive release of cortisol over long periods of time, show a decrease in hippocampal volume through MRI imaging. It presents in verbal declarative memory loss, which is losing the ability to remember facts or lists—this same type of memory loss is also seen in people with PTSD. Along with memory function, the hippocampus plays a role in new learning, and this is negatively impacted by increased cortisol levels.[35]

> More recently, research has begun to focus on other forms of work-related stress. For example, one model views work stress as the outcome of high work demand and low reward. This model both predicts cardiac events and has been correlated with progression of carotid atherosclerosis. Also, low job control, per se, predicts future cardiac events. Taken together, the studies regarding presence of stress at work and subsequent coronary artery disease development have been largely positive, suggesting a strong causal relationship between this form of chronic stress and development of atherosclerosis.[36]

> Stress can stimulate the autonomic sympathetic nervous system to increase vasoconstriction, which can mediate an increase in blood pressure, an increase in blood lipids, disorders in blood clotting, vascular changes, atherogenesis; all, of which, can cause cardiac arrhythmias and subsequent myocardial infarction.[33]

The work you're doing day-to-day matters. Research is clear on the correlation between work-related stress and cardiovascular disease. There is a causal relationship between doing work every day that you find meaningless and soul-wrenching and heart attacks. Do work that's meaningful and soul enriching, not meaningless and soul-wrenching. There will always be stress associated with the work you do, no matter the work, but it's a different stress when it's connected to purpose.

You want to be here as long as you possibly can for your little boy—most likely until he has his own little boy and becomes a dad that kisses his son. Do work that brings you to life so that you can have more life and a longer life. I mean, there's no guarantee that a meteor won't fall from the sky and take you out right now, but that's out of your control. The work you do every day is in your control. Don't smash yourself in the head with a metaphoric meteor by doing work you hate.

As I said earlier, life doesn't need our help in making it hard. Going to a job every day that isn't in line with who we are is a choice. This may be shocking for some to hear, but you can get paid doing work you enjoy. You're much more likely to succeed financially if you find work that's in line with your strengths and gifts.

Again, even doing work you enjoy will bring its own stress, but it's a welcomed stress as opposed to the very unwelcomed stress you feel in the depths of who you are when you think about going back to that fucking job you hate tomorrow morning. If I hit a nerve there, good. That means you need to make some changes.

By this point in reading, you should realize that these changes to better yourself and your situation are also bettering your son's situation. If the stress you're putting yourself through every single day is physically altering your brain and inching you toward cardiac arrest, which it is, you must make a change. There's really no time to waste here.

You don't simply un-alter your brain so that you're a better, more present, and loving dad when you get home from work. As much as you're saying you don't take your work home with you, you are taking your anatomically structurally altered brain home with you.

7

CHAPTER SEVEN

In the last chapter, I talked about a dream I had right before leaving Pittsburgh for California. I took what the dream had shown me as a sign—lighthouse and all. As it turned out, I never actually saw a lighthouse while I was living in California. In fact, I totally forgot about that dream. And I wouldn't remember it until I moved back home to Pittsburgh.

———

When I left for California I took my time and saw as much as I possibly could on the famous Route 66. It took me eleven days total to drive to Los Angeles. There was deep-dish pizza in Chicago, ziplining in Missouri, and then New Mexico—beautiful New Mexico, where I almost didn't leave because I loved it so much. The pueblo-styled architecture with its diverse landscape of mountains and desert and several Starbucks situated right within it was really all I needed. I stayed there for at least two days, and when I was leaving, the sun was peeking just over the mountains in the early morning while hot air balloons filled the sky. On each license plate in New Mexico, "The Land of Enchantment" is written at the bottom. And that description couldn't be more spot on. That's exactly what New Mexico was—especially that morning when I was leaving.

I drove from New Mexico to Las Vegas and by the way, driving through the Mojave Desert with no cell phone service and no forethought to ensure I had a spare tire or at least some Fix-a-Flat was a mostly terrifying experience.

Once I finally landed in California I expected immediate success and a phone call from Oprah. I didn't get a call from Oprah, but I did get an email about being on a show called, "1-on-One with Damon Davis." I'd never heard of it, but when I searched on YouTube, I saw that one of my heroes had been on the show—Les Brown. I'd been listening to Les Brown every day for an entire year leading up to the California move so it felt serendipitous that I'd be featured on the same show he had recently been on. I agreed to do the show and flew to Atlanta a few weeks later to film.

After filming, there was a speaker training event happening the next day that was nearby. The person who hosted the event was the same person that found me on social media and recommended me to the Damon Davis show. Because this person was directly connected to Les Brown, I knew I had to go.

I met a lot of other speakers and coaches who all spoke the same language as me. But something struck me when I told them my story of leaving everything behind in Pittsburgh to move to California—they were surprised. More than surprised, they couldn't believe that I took what we all talked about, listened to, and studied, and actually did it. This hit me because these were my peers in this space, or so I thought, and they saw me as a pariah.

> **"Chase your dreams!"**
> **"Take a chance on yourself!"**
> **"Risk so you can live!"**

When they looked at me, it was like, "Wait, you actually did that stuff?" That was an eye-opening moment. What I learned there is echoed throughout this book—do the things you say you'll do and only teach and lead from the experiences you've had. This couldn't be more important than when you have a little three-foot-tall mini version of yourself looking up at you. You're his role model. Don't fuck it up. Chase your dream and live fully so you can love him fully and help him to chase and understand his dreams. Let the lessons you'll experience be a guide he can use on his path.

When I got back to California, a punch in the throat was waiting for me. The girl I had been dating cheated on me and she fell back into some old patterns that ultimately broke our relationship up. I felt completely broken.

> **"Lighthouses have traditionally been**
> **viewed as symbols of hope and security.**
> **As beacons of light, they provide guidance**
> **for safe passage to sailors and protect not**
> **only their lives but the land nearby."[32]**

A lighthouse always brings you home, directs you on where you need to be.

From where I was standing, there wasn't a lighthouse. I only felt pain. I was shattered. It also turned out that I couldn't afford living in my apartment without another person contributing toward the rent. I picked up a side job of selling life insurance and got sold on the idea that I'd get rich doing it—maybe it was all those damn calls we'd listen to that talked more about Lamborghinis rather than the reality that building a business like that can and very often does take several years. But my heart was broken, I started to miss home, and I thought that if I left USC, I could focus more on getting that Lambo. The truth was, I left USC and barely made more than a handful of sales that didn't even cover gas, let alone rent. And I actually hated the job at USC so I was anxious to get out of there anyway. My thoughts were clouded, and I clearly wasn't making the most informed decisions at the time.

I fell into a deep depression. I remember lying on my apartment floor for over a week without a shirt on, just lost in thoughts, pain, confusion, brokenness, everything. A friend asked me over FaceTime when the last time I wore a shirt was on what was probably day eight of my downward spiral—she called to check on me every few days, and I was always in the same place and always shirtless.

I called Dan's parents, the ones that I'd lived with and that have always been there for me and let our band practice in their basement: "I have sixty-four cents in my account. What should I do? I can't even make it home."

Judy hung up the phone and immediately put $500 in my bank account. I went to the office in my apartment building and said I didn't have a job or any money and had to leave. I sold the few belongings I had there and packed my car once again for a drive across the country, this time with a bit less hope and a lot more brokenness, but also some excitement to be going back home.

It was ten months that I had lived in Los Angeles—I didn't even make it a year. I drove back to Pittsburgh in three days, averaging twelve hours of driving each day. I slept in my car the whole way back, usually in gas station parking lots. When I got back to the Keystone State, I hadn't showered for the three days it took me to drive back because I didn't have money for hotels. I moved into a small room in Dan's parents' house and slowly started to try to collect those shattered, broken pieces of myself.

I was standing in the kitchen one morning wearing gray sweatpants—I did have a shirt on—and it hit me that I couldn't even afford a coffee at Starbucks. Though I was broke and brokenhearted and my chest ached every time I thought about my failed relationship and what seemed to be a failed dream, I kind of laughed at the Starbucks thought. I realized this was as low as I could possibly get. "It's going to make a good story someday," is what I thought.

I sat at the kitchen table, poured coffee into a cup, and made some cereal. When I finished the cereal, just as I was standing up to put the bowl in the sink, I noticed what was painted on the bowl. It was a lighthouse. Painted on the side of the coffee cup . . . another lighthouse. I started looking around the room. The light switch cover was a lighthouse. Most of the paintings were lighthouses. Picture frames were lighthouses. Statues and tiny collectibles—all lighthouses. I was surrounded by lighthouses.

Dan's dad, it turns out, collects anything that looks like a lighthouse. And though I'd been friends with Dan and a part of that family as their unofficial fourth son most of my life, since I was a little boy in kindergarten when I met Dan, I never noticed that everything in that house was a lighthouse. Not even the bowls and dishes we'd used for years. I never noticed that I was completely surrounded by lighthouses in that house.

It's clear that this was the place that I was supposed to go to for healing, a place to reconcile with myself and to clean off the blood from the battle. Seeing those lighthouses brought me hope during one of the most hopeless times of my life.

I went back to the community college, but this time I asked a friend if she'd hire me as an advisor. I only wanted to work with students and not get into the administrative life I was in before I left. Thankfully she gave me a job—Thanks, Tiffany. It was only part-time, but it was a start. I also decided to go back and finish my graduate degree.

My finances took a serious hit from the California dream, and I had to file for bankruptcy. My credit card debt was at $49,000. Making the minimum payment just wasn't going to cut it. I also took my leased car to the dealership and handed them the keys. I told them I was bankrupt and couldn't pay for it anymore. From there, I got a bus pass and downloaded the Uber app.

I vividly remember being in those moments of riding the bus or being in the back of an Uber and thinking to myself, actually it was more of knowing to myself, that this wasn't going to last forever. I knew things would get better. I never stopped thinking and knowing full out that the moment that I was in was temporary. I knew it would pass.

The painful moment you're in right now is also temporary. Your painful moment is going to pass. In fact, it's already coming to pass. You have to believe that so that the pain doesn't swallow you whole. You're needed.

———

The original title of this book was going to be, "Chapter Seven." It's my seventh book, it's been seven years since I wrote my first book, I'm in a new "chapter" of my life in becoming a dad and a husband, and I filed for Chapter Seven Bankruptcy. There was a lot of play on words with the title. But I couldn't connect with the title, and it was the title of this book for two years, but those were two years that I couldn't find focus, motivation, or even a reason to write what you're holding in your hands or reading on your screen right now.

It wasn't until the title changed that the book found its message and its purpose. I commented, "Dads, kiss your sons," on a friend's post on Facebook, and it clicked. I don't even remember what the post was, but I wrote those words and immediately knew what they were and what they meant. It woke me up and caught my heart on fire to write.

Once I got the message, the pages wrote themselves. I think it's important to share our stories and the things we've walked through as well as our triumphs but for what purpose? Who am I hoping to help by sharing this? Is it just some cathartic release for me to talk about all the shitstorms I've endured, or is there a significant meaningful impact and purpose for why I walked through those storms of shit?

When those words flashed in front of me in my mind, I found the "why." I knew exactly who I wanted to talk to, who I wanted to help, and why I walked through all that shit. It wasn't for nothing. It was for something.

DADS, KISS YOUR SONS

I want you to realize that life isn't easy—quite the understatement, right—but that's what makes it kind of incredible. It's a mix of work and surrender that will bring you to live how you want to live. Work looks something like studying more, waking up earlier, going to the gym, learning a new skill, reading. Work is intentionally growing in whichever direction you're being called to grow. So it tends to look different for everyone. But it's always stretching us in the direction of growth.

I discovered this when I came back home from California with my shattered heart. In all that brokenness, the only thing I could really do or have any kind of control over was what I did with myself. I went to the gym every day, sometimes doing two-a-days when the anxiety and pain bit especially hard, and I wrote a blog every day for 106 days in a row. I also wrote another book, called *Karyeator*, which was my first fictional story and is pronounced "Carry-uh-tore"—a play on the word *creator*.

I didn't have control over when my relationship had broken down, but the modicum of control that I did have, and that you have over life, was doing work that stretched me and helped me grow. It's especially important to find meaning- and purpose-filled work when we find ourselves shattered by life. This isn't to ignore those shattered shards lying around you; it's meant to acknowledge them and piece them together into something new.

Surrender is the realization that life is difficult, the control you have over life is the work I just mentioned, and most important, surrender is believing that there is something outside of you and within you that's directing your steps—and directing your steps in love. You can call it God, the Universe, Love itself, or whatever your belief there may be. But this being or entity or energy is calling you and urging you, but never pushing you, to a path that brings you to a more intimate relationship with life's abundance.

If you are a God person, Jesus said, "I have come that they may have life, and have it to the full." Abundance is part of the purpose of Jesus. If you're not a God person, begin to practice believing and seeing life as more abundant than you've been conditioned to think that it is. Success isn't limited to a lucky few—it's connected to the unending current of life available to everyone.

Even with all its mess and misery, life brings love, joy, and fulfillment in an abundance that you don't think you have the capacity to contain within you. And you don't. It's brought in such overflowing abundance that it does exactly that; it overflows. I know this with my whole heart because of the inexplicable pain and brokenness that I've walked through in my life, only to be met with a joy and a love that can truly never be captured in any number of words—and it was when I met my son and held him for the first time. Though I can't explain such an incredible love, it weighed exactly six pounds, six ounces.

You can be shown incredible and horrible darkness just so you can show other people, and yourself, the reality of light. The reality of healing is brought on by the experience of brokenness. You're your story. But more, you're what you do with your story. You're what you do with your story.

THE SCIENCE

There isn't a science section in this chapter. Science can only explain so much. Often, you just have to follow your dreams and let whatever is leading you, lead you.

I cannot emphasize enough the importance of you chasing your dreams so that your son will know and understand the importance and possibility of chasing his own.

8

WE BOTH SWIPED RIGHT

Erin and I met on a dating app called Bumble. When we met, my life was in beautiful ruin. It was a couple years after I moved back to Pittsburgh from California. I was riding the bus and Ubering, basically living out of a backpack and a gym bag, I was working part-time, and I had just finished declaring bankruptcy. I was quite the catch.

At first, I thought Erin's profile was a bot. This isn't some cheesy line, but she was so pretty and such a smoke show that I didn't think she was real. Turns out she was. And she swiped right. Lucky me.

I vividly remember laughing out loud when we were messaging each other through the app. She used to write jokes for comedians when she lived in San Diego, and that humor was coming through with almost every message. She was from Pittsburgh, too, but lived in San Diego for a long time with her ex-husband and two little kids, Cole and Ada. After their marriage dissolved, she moved back to Pittsburgh with her children. We met around two years after that.

Our paths were somewhat similar, and when we met each other for the first time, without an app between us, it felt like we were just picking up where we left off, even though this was our first time meeting. And it was after only six months of dating that we decided to move in together. Not long after that, she said this:

"I've taken three tests, and they're all positive!"

Erin's voice came blaring through the phone as I was driving home from class for my graduate program, saying—well, more frantically screaming, really—that I was going to be a dad. She was beside herself. I assured her that things would be alright. She relaxed, we went to dinner, and everything was fine—until it set in with me two weeks later and I started losing my damn mind.

All of a sudden, I was terrified. I didn't have a dad growing up, I didn't know what dads did—how could I possibly be a dad? The only thing that scared me more was when I found out we were going to have a boy. Remember what I said before about hating sports? HOW THE HELL WAS I GOING TO RAISE A BOY? I was raised by three women—my aunt, my grandmother, and my mom. Not only did I not know what dads did, but I didn't even know what dudes did!

Joking aside, I'm ashamed to say that in those panicked early moments, I didn't want Erin to go through with the pregnancy, and if she did, I wanted to give the baby up for adoption.

Saying that now makes me want to fucking puke. I can't believe that I was ever in that frame of mind. It's so completely opposite of me that I barely recognize the memory.

I went back and forth with whether or not to write this because someday my little homie won't be so little, and he'll probably read this. But I think it's critical for men to know, men that are about to be first-time dads specifically, that these thoughts can and likely will come in and grip you. And it's OK. I became the father I never knew could even exist to my little boy, and this is where I fucking started. I started at letting fear take total control of my thoughts and not even thinking for a second of the possibility of how amazing it would actually be to become a father. I was *only* terrified. I was *only* afraid. I was *only* listening to fear. That was the only voice I could hear.

All of this was happening in my head after that first visit to the doctor that showed Erin was indeed pregnant. But it was still too early to tell if it was what's called a *viable pregnancy*, meaning that the fetus has a chance of further development and survival. Until they can hear the heartbeat, which wouldn't be for a couple more weeks, the pregnancy is not yet labeled as viable. During those couple weeks, I was a mental case and paralyzed in fear, thinking thoughts that, again, make me want to fucking puke. This is where my cousin Vicky came in.

Vicky, my aunt Doe's daughter and Kai's Nunnie, the person that pointed me in the direction of who my real dad was, the fourth woman who raised me, and the other greatest person I've ever known, dismantled every fear I had in an instant. It was Christmas in 2019 when Erin and I were at Vicky's house and told her we were going to have a baby. Her excitement and the endless stream of joyful tears running down her face made me realize that this was OK. It was more than OK. It was exciting and amazing and beautiful. Somehow in my mind I wasn't a thirty-four-year-old educated and working adult about to have a baby with a woman I was in a loving and mature relationship with; I was a scared sixteen-year-old that got my girlfriend pregnant. Vicky's joy showed me that I wasn't "in trouble." What a strange place to be, but that's where I was.

That crippling and embarrassing fear that had latched onto me for weeks dissolved faster than it had come on. When we went back to the doctor for the next checkup, we heard his heartbeat, and I fell in love.

To you, Kai, I want you to know that I never didn't want *you*. I was giving into a fear that it was me that you would never want. How could you? What did I have to offer a son? I was unqualified to the highest degree. I was also selfish and fearful of a long-term commitment to Erin. Even though we fell immediately in love with one another, I started to let fear dictate my thoughts there as well. And the thing is, when I was in that moment of fear, it wasn't about you—I didn't know you—it was about me. How could I rise to this occasion? I didn't think I could. I just totally gave into fear.

Thankfully, though, I did come out of it. And from that moment, and the moment of hearing your heartbeat, I knew I would do everything and be everything that you needed me to be. I knew I'd love you and carry you and care for you. Before you were born, I knew that I would always be there and present in your life. And the moment you were in my arms . . . there aren't any words, Kai. Just like I wrote in your song:

The moment you were born was
the moment I came to life
Thank you, thank you for being my baby, Kai

How can you put words to a love so strong that it brings you to life? You can't. And just as I say further in that song and over you every night—you are strong, you are safe, you are secure, you are brave, you are blessed and highly favored, and you are loved beyond anything you can ever imagine. Please forgive me for not knowing my place those first few weeks before hearing your heartbeat. I love you so much, little boy. I love you so much.

———

When Kai was born, I felt a love like words can't hope to capture. I learned that I didn't need to have received the love that I was so easily able to give to my son. Just because you didn't see something from your past does not mean that you can't know that thing in your present. The gift of becoming a parent brings with it a capacity to love as you have never known before. A love that can make you the best person you can possibly be. A love that you would lift mountains and drink oceans for. The love that you experience as a parent is the greatest gift that this life offers us—it's freeing, it's pure, and it is unmatched.

When I was allowing my thoughts to operate out of only fear, I worried about everything. I thought I needed at least seven figures in my savings account before I could be a good dad. I thought I needed to have the bestseller written and sold before I could be a good dad. I thought that having a baby would force me to give up on my dreams. The reality of all that is, you don't need every single duck in a row before you become a dad, because as I said before, those ducks don't exist anyway. And the part about dreams? Well, that little one will inspire you more than you could have ever hoped to have been inspired before they were born. Along with this explosion of inspiration and deepened purpose to pursue your dreams, you will find once again that you have new dreams that you never knew existed until right now, Dad.

To you men who are finding yourselves in that current state of paralyzing fear at the prospect of becoming a father, this has hopefully helped you. But if you're still there, it's OK. It's not going to go away until it goes away. My advice here is simple . . . stick around until it goes away. I promise that it will. I think that not enough men have been told to simply stick around until the discomfort dissipates. Stick around.

THE SCIENCE

Apparently, this fear of becoming a father is not a unique experience bestowed only unto me. I'm an example of many who share a similar crippling anxiety as they approach fatherhood—though the many seem to be few, as reflected in the limited body of research available on this.

> The modern gender constructs of "maleness" suggest that men should be strong and self-confident, which does not encourage fathers-to-be to express fears about their own capabilities. Men may question the legitimacy of their psychological experiences during the perinatal period as they view themselves in a supportive role to their partner and consequently are reluctant to express and com-

municate their fears around birth and fatherhood. Fatherhood, even when it is desired and
planned for, can be a difficult time of transi-
tion for some men, negatively impacting their
mental health, resulting in stress, anxiety,
and depression.[37]

There actually doesn't appear to be much research done
on this. In fact, what I cited above is from 2021, so it's fairly
recent. That same article goes on to say the following:

**"Limited research has explored paternal
fear of childbirth (FOC) using validated
screening tools and there is a lack of
consistent definition of paternal FOC
across the literature, making the true
incidence rate difficult to determine."** [37]

There is fear associated with explaining your fear of becoming a dad. Men are to be strong, certain, and courageous
leaders. Not fearful. Because of flawed cultural mores project-
ed onto men, they fear speaking up about their fears. So even
in 2021, there's research explaining that there isn't much research done on this fear of becoming a father.

It's as if those flawed thinking patterns and masculine ex-
pectancies kick into overdrive when we learn we're about to
become a dad. Now there's no choice; it's either lead or leave.
The color of the situation turns black and white.

In opening up and explaining the debilitating fear that
we're facing, we find support. We find others that can hold
us up when our legs give out beneath the weight of fearful

thoughts that are flooding our minds. We have others that can help us hold our legs in place when fear is pushing us to leave.

> **"Fathers experience psychological distress
> in the perinatal period but question
> the legitimacy of their experiences.
> Men may thus be reluctant to express
> their support needs or seek help amid
> concerns that to do so would detract
> from their partner's needs."[38]**

Much of the focus, understandably so, is on the mother during pregnancy. It is the mother who carries the child for nine months and deals with the incredible changes taking place within her body that she has zero control over.

When Erin was pregnant with Kai, she had hyperemesis gravidarum—which is morning sickness times a thousand. This is not an exaggeration; Erin puked on average eight to ten times per day for eight months straight. Every single day for *eight months*. The purple bucket next to our bed got a lot of mileage during that time. She could barely eat or drink anything, and what she did hold down was just enough to keep her out of a hospital bed. It was an extremely difficult pregnancy on her physical health but also, obviously, her mental health. I really didn't know and still don't know how she got through all of that. All I can come up with is that she's a fucking warrior.

So, with all of that, did I really have ground to stand on when I said something like, "I don't know about this. I'm scared"? Seems kind of comical, and it is, to a point, but the reality is that the mental strain that I experienced was just as relevant and mattered just as much as those extreme physical and mental challenges that she was enduring. And if I wanted to be a better support for her, which I absolutely needed to be, then I needed to ensure there was support for me. I needed to voice the fears that I was feeling. And I did.

> The prevalence of fathers' depression and anxiety in the perinatal period (i.e., from conception to one year after birth) is approximately 5–10 percent, and 5–15 percent, respectively; their children face increased risk of adverse emotional and behavioral outcomes, independent of maternal mental health. Critically, fathers can be protective against the development of maternal perinatal mental health problems and their effects on child outcomes. Preventing and treating paternal mental health problems and promoting paternal psychological well-being may therefore benefit the family as a whole.[38]

In wanting to be there for your partner, you have to first be there for yourself. You have to come to a place where you can admit the fear you're feeling and find the support you need to work through it. Be as honest with yourself and your supports as possible, no matter how shameful those admissions may seem. I promise you, the thoughts you're thinking are not your own. They're making you think that you're something other than who you are, so how can they be yours? Those thoughts belong to Fear. Do all that you can not to allow fear to dictate your movements. And I can tell you this, you can't do it alone.

There was an important word used in the quote above, "preventing." Don't wait until the problem you're facing becomes so insurmountable you can't surmount it. Practice preventative measures that keep your mental health in check, like talking with a counselor or therapist before you think you need to talk to a counselor or therapist.

Even if you've already walked the dad road before, maybe it's been a while and you're not sure you can do it again. You're still susceptible to that very human experience of fear and the worthless thoughts that come with it. You're still susceptible to allowing fear to fuck you up. Don't let fear fuck you up. Get in front of it. Like I mentioned before, stick around, Dad.

9

THE DAY I WOKE UP AS A BLACK MAN

"Get out of my hedges, you little nigger!"

Being told my whole life that I was Italian, this bigoted threat came as kind of a surprise when it was said to me. I was maybe ten or eleven years old and playing outside with my friends on a summer day. For some reason I decided to sit in someone's hedges, either to hide while playing a game, or maybe I was just being an asshole kid and sat in someone's hedges. But when the homeowner that I hadn't seen screamed the above slur toward me, I didn't know who he was talking to. I and all my friends were white.

I mentioned before that when I was a baby or a toddler, people would sometimes ask my mom if I was mixed race, and she would lose her mind on them. My mom was racist and referred to black people with that same derogatory term said above. I was raised to believe that black people were both bad and less than. And then one day, when I was twenty-five, I discovered that I was black.

When I tell people that I thought I was Italian most of my life and didn't know I was black, they usually ask if I ever looked into a mirror or knew what black people looked like. Even if you don't adopt the beliefs of your parents, much of what they said daily will stick with you and ingrain itself within the foundation of who you are. So even though I didn't grow up to be a racist, there was still some stuff in me that I needed to unlearn.

I mean, when you hear every day during your formative years that a specific group is bad for this reason or that reason, even when you get old enough to realize how inaccurate a thing like that can be, there's still a light film leftover in your thinking, even if it's subconscious. Those counterfactual presuppositions about black people, whether I like it or not, and I don't, were mixed in with the cement of the foundation that formed my early thinking. Fire's hot, ice is cold, don't eat things with a Mr. Yuck sticker, black people are bad.

I've been working in higher education for over a decade. I've been a student success coach, math instructor, scholarship coordinator, tutor, advisor, and tenure-track faculty member. I've worked at some of the most prestigious and well-respected universities in the country, including Carnegie Mellon University (CMU), the University of Pittsburgh (Pitt), and the University of Southern California (USC), and I've been able to provide for myself and my family while doing work that I enjoy.

Every single great opportunity that led to the next great opportunity was by someone making a call and opening the door for me. And every single one of those people that have done those things for me were black. If not for them, I would never have had the career in higher education that I've had, and I likely wouldn't even be writing this book.

It's not that I came into adulthood with the thought or expectation that black people had to do things for me to prove themselves. But I found that my experience with black people was far different than how my mom painted the picture when I was growing up.

While my mom painted this picture, my aunt was painting another one. My aunt Doe lived in the projects. Every neighbor was black. She was certainly the minority in that community. And she was friends with every person in that community. It was a conflicting experience for me to live with my mom but spend a ton of time with my aunt when they were both on very different sides of the fence. Thankfully it was always my aunt that had the greater influence on me, and basically every experience I'd ever had in life would always fly in the face of the nonsense and hatred my mom would spew while confirming the goodness of my aunt.

It's because of my aunt that I grew up without a hate-filled heart. But it still sucks that I had to battle the thought out of my mind, influenced by my mom, that maybe black people were somehow different than me and in a lesser way. It's especially fucking stupid when you find out you're black. That was what I had to unlearn. First, I had to confront the reality that that thought may be something I held consciously, subconsciously, or both, and then burn it from my being. It's easy to get rid of a thought like that because it's bullshit. It doesn't make sense. Hating a person can make some sense, hating a people makes no fucking sense.

Your identity says, "This is who I am." And we attach ourselves so tightly to that idea of an identity, or the ideas that culminate to make our identity, that we can miss out on growth. We miss out on seeing that there's better within us and those around us, and we miss out on correcting things within us that need to be corrected. We miss out on growth because we say things to ourselves like, "I'm not a depressed person, I'm not an anxious person." And you may never have been, but now you are because life changes. I wasn't black for the first twenty-five years of my life, and then I was. My identity shifted, and I had to really examine what that meant to me. Was it bad like my mom surely made it seem? Was it good? What was it?

However I chose to see it, this was my new reality. And by this point, especially having had enough people throughout my life say that there had to be some black in me, I wasn't entirely stunned by the revelation. I think I was just angry with my mom that she had implanted this idea in my head that there was anything of a difference between two groups of people, while the whole time I was made up of both groups!

She's an asshole for that. But I do forgive her. I think you can think someone's an asshole and still forgive them at the same time.

Racism is taught to kids, and racism isn't always screaming the N-word or wearing white hoods or flying Confederate flags. Racism can be subtle, like thinking that one group of people just aren't quite as good as another group. I really fucking hate that that's something I know, and I almost wish I could unknow it. But it does open the conversation that racism isn't always blaring and is often subtle, and this experience has made me very aware of that.

My son will likely experience some things in his life that I'd rather he didn't, and we will have some uncomfortable conversations as he gets older. But the more that I know, accept, and seek to understand myself, the better I'll be able to help him know and understand himself. He will never be afraid to talk to me about things that he's afraid of. He will know that no question or conversation is ever off the table.

To you dads, what are some things about you that you're afraid to see? What are some things that you know are within you that need to be brought out to the open? Write it all down and find support to help you work through and understand that fucking mess. And it's OK, we're literally all dealing with something of a fucking mess—the only thing that distinguishes those of us on a better path is that we're open to walking it by way of being painfully honest with ourselves and talking about it. I told you before to sit with your discomfort. But you don't have to sit with it alone.

THE SCIENCE

This is another chapter that doesn't have a true science section. Explaining this part of my life and upbringing is a very hard and vulnerable thing to do. When I came to find out that my real dad was black, it was jarring. Not because I hated black people, but because my mom did. So I really had to sit with myself and examine if there were any racist beliefs residing within me. Not that I hadn't thought about this before, but it wasn't something I thought much about. Probably because I'm not racist.

Even though my mom was how she was, I was raised in a black neighborhood and had black friends. And the most important people in my life who were also raising me didn't have a drop of racism in them. They also probably knew that I was black and didn't say anything for fear of having my mom lose her mind on them and rip me out of their lives—the same threat she gave if they were to take me around the person she said was my dad.

What a fuckin' mess.

Though, like I mentioned above, racism isn't always blaring, and I certainly wasn't looking for sign-up sheets to join white supremacist groups before I found out I was black. But I really needed to sit with myself to determine what this meant to me—if anything. I was confronted with a major life shift that brought a whole new truth to me that I didn't know before. And I acknowledged that there was a feeling that black people were at least different than me. And that sucks. And it's something that I easily walked away from the moment I saw that it was there all those years ago.

We have to realize some uncomfortable things about ourselves at times and do all we can to change them and fix them. We have to shine a light on ourselves, every single part of ourselves, to know who we really are and what we need to change. This happened to me more than ten years ago when I was twenty-five. I confronted the truth of my heritage, confronted the truth of any of the thoughts that still permeated my mind from my youth living with a racist mom, and became a better and fuller person.

I'm so glad I was able to do that for myself and for my son. Imagine having unknown and deeply buried racist beliefs when your own son, who you love more than life, is on the other end of those broken and terrible thoughts. That also makes me want to puke.

10

BECOMING THE ALCHEMIST

When Kai was born, I felt so much in me come to life. I knew in that moment, holding that baby, that everything I'd do for the rest of my life would be for him. I also remember seeing him sleeping while Erin was sleeping in the hospital bed next to him and feeling like I'd just started a new job. I was terrified of him waking up from his nap because I really didn't know what the hell I was doing. It felt like I was in a new job hoping that a customer wouldn't come through the door because I truly didn't know what I was doing. There I was, six feet tall, 270 pounds, tattooed, and terrified of a twenty-one-inch long, six-pound, six-ounce Kai baby.

> **"I'm going to show you this once."**
> **—the nurse changing newborn Kai's diaper**

After I watched and learned how to work a diaper, I've been slinging them ever since. Two years running, and I'm a damn beast at changing di-pees.

Making bottles, check.

Cleaning bottles, check.

Almost not a single night of sleeping straight through the night in two years, double check.

I've given Kai a bath almost every single night since he was born, except for a small handful of times when he was either sleeping at his Nunnie's or his Grandma Judy came over to give him one. And I always miss it when I'm not giving him a bath. Just watching the bath time progression in him has been something I'll always cherish.

When he was tiny newborn Kai, he'd lie in his little tub while I gently poured water over him and cleaned all his chonky rolls. Erin taught me how to clean him, and then it just kind of became our thing. Just me and Kai. Eventually he didn't need the little tub anymore, and he progressed to what was more of a seat, and eventually it was just him and the big tub. To him it probably felt like an ocean. For me, it became an ongoing battle to keep him from drinking the bath water he'd likely just peed in. And in almost two years, we've only had one number two incident in the tub.

Before he could really walk, I'd pick him up and say, "IS IT BATHTIME?" in a wildly overexcited voice to get him to laugh, and then I'd put him in the water. Now, because he loves bath time so much and he can get himself in the tub without my help, it's hilarious to watch him run his little naked butt into the bathroom and climb into the tub with a big smile on his face and as many toys as he can manage to play with at one time. I still pick him up sometimes and crazily yell, "IS IT BATHTIME?" which makes him laugh his little ass off. God, I love being a dad.

This is the kind of presence our sons need from us, dads. They need us to be there doing these daily tasks but with excitement and enthusiasm and love. And I have to tell you, that's not something that you'll necessarily have to work at. Even on the most stressful of days when nothing else is working, there's bath time. Even when he's not in a great mood and miserable during bath time, it feeds your heart to care for him.

Maybe you're thinking you don't have time—to which I'll say this: bullshit. When Kai was born, I was working full-time at one college and part-time at another college, had one more year of graduate school to go, and was getting married the next month. Now, I'm done with grad school, I still work two jobs, I'm extremely dedicated to writing, I'm still married to my best friend with two great stepkids, we bought a house, and I go to the gym. I never miss bath time. My advice to you is to never miss bath time. Even if you miss it a couple times, say to yourself and keep that belief in your mind that you never miss bath time.

I never miss bath time. I'll never miss bath time.

This also works with going to the gym. Even if I miss a few days, in my mind I have the cemented belief that I go to the gym every day. Because of this thinking, I show up far more often than I otherwise would if my thoughts were anything other than, *I do this every day*. A lot of dads die way too young from preventative diseases, and our sons need us. We have to eat less pizza and go to the gym more, even though pizza is fucking delicious and the gym sucks.

I've truly loved and continue to love that baby more than words can catch. I've said that so many times, but it bears repeating again and again and again. It's overwhelming to know what our hearts are capable of. I had that strange fear during those first few frantic weeks of learning I'd be a dad that I would no longer be able to continue chasing my dreams. How crazy that is to look back on now with Kai being so clearly a beautiful dream coming true that I never knew I had. New dreams live within your heart that you don't realize are there, and it will absolutely take your breath away when they're born.

I had a dream to move to California. It burned in me to go, and eventually I did. I sold everything I owned and journeyed west. I got the shit kicked out of me. I ran out of money. I got my heart broken. Everything started pointing to going back to Pittsburgh, including my heart. And the whole time while walking through this, I was thinking of the story *The Alchemist*, by Paulo Coelho—undoubtedly my favorite book.

The parallels between that story and mine were almost frightening. *Spoiler alert ahead.* Santiago had a dream that his treasure was in the Pyramids of Egypt. I dreamed that mine was in California. Santiago loses all his money the moment he sets foot in the new land he'd journeyed to and almost has to go back home to Spain until he finds work with a crystal merchant. I was out of money, I almost had to go back to Pittsburgh, and then right at that last possible moment, I got the job with USC.

Santiago continues forward. I continued forward.

Eventually Santiago physically gets the shit kicked out of him, which reveals that his treasure is right where he started in Spain, so he leaves the Pyramids and travels back home. I got the shit kicked out of me emotionally and began feeling a tug on my heart to go back home to Pittsburgh. After my emotional beating, limping around with a broken heart, this story of Santiago jumped into my head. I started to think that maybe my treasure was back home in Pittsburgh just as Santiago's was back in Spain.

At the time, I was selling life insurance and started to think that I had a warmer market back home. Maybe that's where I would find my riches and Lambos. That wasn't the case, and I didn't find massive cash flow in life insurance sales. In fact, I hated sales but wouldn't let myself quit until I got my "close ratio" to 80 percent. Once I did that, I knew I was quitting because I hated it and not just because it was difficult and it sucked. It was difficult and it did suck, but that wasn't why I quit. I quit because it wasn't in line at all, for even a second, with my heart.

So I didn't find treasure in a warm market selling life insurance. I found Erin. Not long after that, I found fatherhood. And not long after that, I wrote this book. It turned out that I was right, and just like Santiago, my riches really were where I started. Just like Santiago, I had to travel thousands of miles and walk through what seemed to be endless shitstorms to finally get to my treasure. In a way, I sort of became the alchemist.

If you're thinking that maybe I'm looking too deep into this story and just wanting to see myself in it, you may be right. But one other thing that Santiago does in the book is an unimaginable feat by turning himself into the wind. I've never turned myself into the wind, but when Erin bought me that ancestry kit, it was clear that I had turned into a black man. So fuck you, I am the alchemist.

THE SCIENCE

Alchemy is often considered a precursor to modern chemistry. Until somewhat recently, much of the history of this ancient science has been considered, especially by the scholarly community, as more fairy tale and fiction—especially with its primary pursuits being the transmutation of various metals into gold and creating an elixir that brings eternal life.[39]

Though, in pursuing these interests, the alchemists began to form the foundation of chemistry by way of breaking down and understanding various chemical properties and interactions between elements. This can be linked to modern industries such as metallurgy and the production of paints, inks, dyes, and cosmetics.

Tracing back to ancient Egypt, the alchemist and physician Hayyan introduced chemical methodologies used today such as crystallization, sublimation and evaporation, synthesis of acids, and distillation. Hayyan applied this to improving the manufacturing of things such as glassmaking, steel development, and other advancements in major industries that are still with us today.[39]

In Renaissance Europe, alchemy found popularity among the scientific elites we now credit with so much of our modern understanding of science. Isaac Newton, who watched an apple fall from a tree and created calculus, and Robert Boyle, known for Boyle's Law in chemistry, were both known to study alchemy.

Boyle believed that transmutation was simply a matter of rearranging particles of an element. This belief held true when, in 1919, Earnest Rutherford aimed alpha particles at nitrogen atoms, which transformed nitrogen to oxygen. This was the first man-made nuclear reaction and pinned Rutherford as the father of nuclear physics.[39]

Modern scientists seemed to extract the mysticism from alchemy and called it chemistry, almost as if that were a chemical process itself. We do this with a lot of things in life. We only want to look for what's "real" and what we can tangibly grasp.

The elixir of life may not have been created, but is there nothing mystical in merging elements and compounds to create medicines that increase the quality of life, rid us of disease, and prevent new ones from occurring? Why are we so quick to discredit or try to explain away that which is truly magical when it occurs before our eyes?

Maybe we should stop believing magic isn't something that can exist or does exist within the very real things we see every day. We should, to steal a chemistry term, try to dissociate ourselves from familiarity and how it shapes our perception—rather looking at these things that are familiar as if they're new. Then we'll see things we haven't seen before in the things we've already seen before.

Your life is no longer that broken-down and dilapidated hopeless structure that it may have once been. Flawed childhoods and lying parents, that's all gone now. Your life has found its own transmutation into something truly magnificent and truly pure. Look into your little boy's eyes, and that's where you'll see it. That's where you'll find something of your own philosopher's stone.

//

WE GOT MARRIED AT STARBUCKS

The Waterfront is an area near our house that has shops, restaurants, an outdoor promenade, a movie theater, and a great bike trail that runs along the river. The Waterfront is our second home. It's where I go to write and drink coffee in the morning. It's where we take Kai for long walks on the trail or to Barnes & Noble, where he sits at a table and sips my iced coffee; or to Starbucks, where they give him cake pops; or to Primanti Bros., where he eats fish sandwiches and french fries; or to the candy store, where he eats his mom's rock candy.

It's our spot. In fact, when the world was really in the grips of the pandemic, Erin and I got married at the Waterfront. It was outside near a water fountain that happened to be right next to Starbucks. So we did kind of get married at Starbucks. It was on a perfect sunny day in late September 2020 that our friend, John Fetterman, who at the time was the Lieutenant Governor of Pennsylvania, married us. People were there, people were masked, and it was perfect. We had tacos after. Who has a wedding ceremony at Starbucks and a reception over tacos and enchiladas? Us.

A few weeks ago, we were in the Waterfront, as usual, and a stranger came up to me to tell me that I was a great dad. He was an older guy and said that I'm always there doing things with my son that not a lot of men do with their little boys.

Now, believe me when I say that my dream and goal is for this book to hit every bestseller list that there is. I'll gladly and gratefully take whatever awards anyone would like to give me for this work. And my gratitude will truly be immeasurable. I mean that sincerely.

But the absolute most important compliment I can ever hope and wish to receive that matters above anything else and the one that I absolutely strive for is that I'm a good dad.

1 *New York Times* Bestselling Author is a beautiful title. But being a good dad is the one that matters more. So when this man said this to me, it truly meant everything.

There are some practices that I do that I believe will make you a better dad. These are practices that start with me so that I'm better for myself, which allows me to be better for my son. The purpose of the stories I've shared and the research I've looked at is to get as many men as possible to kiss their sons and allow themselves to be open and beautifully vulnerable to the reality of being fully human. Scared, sad, happy, insecure, brave, loved, in love—everything, the whole spectrum of human. Little boys need their daddies, and, dads, you need your little boys.

I can't stress enough within this text the importance of working on yourself so that you continue to grow in a direction that makes you more present, more caring, more understanding, more loving, and more of a leader—all the things your little boy needs from you.

John Maxwell explains that leadership is influence. You have massive—and I mean *massive*—influence on your sons. And what expands that influence is the action you consistently take. Your life is a demonstration to your son. And let's be real, it's not only a demonstration to your son, but also all those around you that you love and care about. Who you say you are and who you act you are hopefully line up.

1. WORK ON YOUR THOUGHTS

We've heard this a million times, "As a man thinks in his heart, so he is." It's out of Proverbs in the Bible, and the reason we've heard it so much is that it's damn important. Brian Tracy says it over and over in one of his recordings, "You are what you think about most of the time."

Thoughts consume us. All of us. Every day we are absolutely consumed with thought. Thoughts bring about emotion, and emotion brings about action. Action is really the only defining force of who you are. It's what you do that makes you. And its root, where it begins, is thought. How incredibly important our thoughts are that they should dictate the actions we take in life.

Do we demonstrate present, loving, and kind actions toward our sons? Or are we neglectful, even abusive? If you say that your thoughts get the best of you, congratulations, you're human. You do what all humans do—act in congruency with the thoughts that you think about most of the time.

But you can get ahead of your thoughts and get the better of them before they get the better of you. You want to start listening and reading things that bring life to your mind. And after you've done that, pay attention to your thoughts. Practice countering what they're saying to you. But you have to be quick and realize that you're thinking some shitty thoughts. You're so used to thinking you suck that you don't even realize you're thinking that you suck.

"I'll never finish this degree."
"I will absolutely complete my degree."
"I can't trust people because of my past."
"I'm learning every day to trust
better because my past has shown
me how important trust is."
"I suck."
"I don't suck."

My suggestion is to listen to more positive things than you probably are now, but it doesn't have to be every moment of every day. You'll start to get pretty annoying if you get too positive. This is to help you start to think better, so you can believe better, so you can live better. I'm simply saying, maybe while driving to work or if you're at the gym, put on a self-development podcast or YouTube video. And read at least thirty minutes every day. You have the time. Trust me.

Along with the countering practice, introduce the practice of affirming the things you *do* want in life. Do this without judgment of yourself. You'll usually only judge yourself here because you're somehow thinking the maddening thought of "What will other people think of what I think?" It's kind of hilarious how insane we are, isn't it?

Some of you may think affirmations are stupid or cliché, and that's alright. Just give yourself a chance to be open for two seconds and try these practices. The affirmations are more than just saying the things you think you should say to yourself—you have to believe them. Or do your best to put it in your mind that you believe them.

When you're affirming these things you want in your life, truly imagine them as your current reality. Feel all the feels that come along with those amazing things you want to have and experience. Feel the wind on your face as you're sitting on your patio in Laguna Beach. Smell the fresh leather of the Rolls-Royce you're in. Feel the relief of paying off your student loans in full and the freedom of having no debt. Feel the fullness of accomplishing that project you're working on or the degree you're finishing. Your graduation date may be years down the line, but allow yourself to feel that accomplishment now while you're doing the hard stuff to get there.

Imagining things in this way solidifies in your mind and your being that these things will absolutely come to pass because, to you, they already have.

Words give life, but words can also bring death. Words are so much more powerful than you may think they are. This affirmation practice will put you in more of the driver's seat of your thoughts and build newer neurological paths to thinking better, even feeling better. Remember, it's a practice, so you have to practice it.

"I am abundant, and I attract abundance."
"Good things happen to me."
"I like myself."
"I am attracting opportunity."
"I am attracting money."

I speak the following affirmations over Kai into the mirror every night after bath time right before we brush his teeth:

"You're strong, you're safe, you're secure, you're brave, you're blessed and highly favored. You're covered in the blood of Jesus, you're healthy, you're kind, and you're so so loved. You were born into abundance. You were born into blessing. You are abundant and you are a blessing. And Mommy and Daddy love you so so much, Kai. I love you. I love you. I love you."

Don't let the Jesus blood thing freak you out if you're not a God person. It's just another way of saying he's baptized in God's love and forgiveness.

Words have incredible power. They can build up or tear apart with the same ferocity. I'm planting these seeds of powerful words in Kai that will hopefully guide his thoughts throughout the days of his life, especially when he faces a challenge.

To simplify this whole section, speak against what you don't want and speak about the things you do want.

2. BUILD DISCIPLINE

Read more. If you have gotten this far in the book, you're defeating the statistic that says about a quarter of American adults, or 23 percent, haven't read a whole book or even part of a book in the last year.[41] Take thirty minutes, at a minimum, to read every day. It's a great practice to get in that's easy and shows you that you have more control over yourself than you tend to think you have.

Thomas Corley is the author of *Rich Habits: The Daily Success Habits of Wealthy Individuals*. In the book, he defines the rich as those who have an annual income of $160,000 or more with a net worth of $3.2 million or more, and the poor as those who have an annual income of $35,000 or less and a net worth of $5,000 or less. Corley writes the following about reading, "The rich are voracious readers on how to improve themselves." Corley shows that 88 percent of those identified as rich read thirty minutes or more each day. He also found that only 2 percent of those identified as poor read this way.[40]

It's sad to note that during times of economic downturn, there seems to be a correlation between that and domestic violence. There's research showing that the rate of domestic violence is 9.5 percent in couples experiencing high levels of financial strain as compared to 2.7 percent in couples not feeling financial strain.[42]

Reading and the continuation of learning, even if you have a master's degree or a doctorate, positions you to build a more sound financial life and one that isn't affected as badly during times of economic duress. You can and will build the life you dream of for your family. But it's reading and self-education that are critical to that end.

Get yourself to a place where you don't even have to make the decision to do the things you know you need to do daily. Let reading and other needed habits just become part of your day.

I mentioned that so many men die early of preventative diseases. A leading one is heart disease, which men develop ten years earlier than women on average.[43] About 1 in 13 white men and 1 in 14 black men have coronary artery disease.[44]

This is very real. You're not immortal, and there are practices that need to be put in place to increase your chances of seeing your loved little boy grow into a loving man. Read more, educate yourself, and move more.

Discipline is achieved by doing what you say you're going to do more often than you don't do what you say you're going to do. Your disciplines, though, have to be built around purpose. That's the key to maintaining them.

Tony Robbins says people don't get what they want, they get what they have to have. He explains that when your *should* becomes a *must*, that's when real change occurs. And the only way you get from *should* to *must* is by tying it to purpose.

Sure, everyone *should* work out more, but you and I *must* work out more because our little boys need us. I will do everything I possibly can to make my experience with my son and his experience with me as full as possible, and I will be here as long as possible to enjoy the fullness of that experience.

3. EAT BETTER

I love pizza. Like really love pizza. I could eat pizza every single day for the rest of my life, which probably wouldn't actually be very long if I maintained that practice. That's the world I wish I lived in. But it's not. And I feel like complete trash when I'm on a stretch of bad eating.

It's great in the moment, and I love the rush of dopamine that floods my brain with each cheesy slice I eat. But I don't love the underlying arteries being clogged with fat or the physical and mental fatigue I feel with the sugar crash caused by the overabundance of insulin running through me. So it's a moment of feeling great that turns into many moments of feeling terrible.

This obviously ties in with the above disciplines of exercise and self-education. But since this isn't a book on dieting, I'll leave you with this: eat less shitty than you're currently eating. Still eat pizza on days, just not every day. Cook more, McD's less.

4. LEAN INTO THE DIFFICULT

This is absolutely necessary to repeat: men, stick around. It can be terrifying to become a dad. Your point of reference is usually a fucked-up past. But that past does not need to be repeated, and if you so desire, it will not be repeated. Breaking generational curses is pretty easy. Just don't do the dumb shit that your parents did to you or the dumb shit their parents did to them or the dumb shit their parents did to them and so on. Just don't do it.

If you have a hard time with some of the behaviors you saw growing up, get the help you need to stop doing them. And definitely don't do them in front of or to your child.

You're likely aware, at this point in the game, that life isn't exactly a breeze. Every person who has ever been or ever will be has had and will have problems and hurdles to overcome. And if we really look at the patterns of those things that are difficult, there's often a good payoff on the other side of them.

Much of our generation and the generations coming up are kind of soft. Afraid to hurt. Afraid of discomfort. And again, by no means do I consider myself some kind of ba-dass, but I have walked through some shit and have engaged in battle with those asshole demons that have haunted me. I do know the power and even the privilege of walking through hard times. People think there's a pot of gold at the end of a rainbow, but I'm convinced that it's at the end of a shitstorm.

You've heard it before to get comfortable being uncomfortable. Les Brown has a great quote that says, "If you do what is easy, your life will be hard, but if you do what is hard, your life will be easy."

It's easy to hit the dollar menu and the drive-thru.

But it's hard to have strokes and heart attacks.

It's hard to eat more salad and less pizza. Trust me.

But it's easy to run after my two-year-old without obstructed arteries.

5. GET AROUND THE RIGHT PEOPLE

Your associations and the people you spend the most time with are key to your success or key to keeping you in ruin. If you're around a bunch of fuckups, you'll fall into the flow of being a fuckup. If you're not around anyone at all, you'll start listening to yourself way too much. Get around people pushing themselves to be better that look at you with the same expectation.

When you've listened to speaker after speaker that has had incredible success in their lives and they're teaching on the things they do and have done to achieve these stratospheric levels of success, there are a few running themes throughout their messages. This is one of them.

Being around the right people will position you to accomplish the things you want to accomplish and some things you don't even realize you want to accomplish.

People that lend to your growth and encourage it are the ones you're looking for. People that diminish you and your hope are the ones to look out for. Stay away from them. Sometimes those are the people closest to you—often biologically, but sometimes not. Either way, get away from those that are stuck, happy about being stuck, and want you to stay stuck with them.

Get around those that are stuck, want to get unstuck, want to see you get unstuck, or have already gotten themselves unstuck. The company you keep will keep you. Decide where it is that you'd like that company to keep you.

———

You likely notice that the above list aimed at making you a better dad is entirely focused on you. Ed Mylett is an entrepreneur and author and hosts my favorite podcast. He has a great quote that says, "One of the most insidious forms of child neglect is a parent who doesn't chase their dreams and potential." Damn. Let that seep into you for a second.

To not do these things is harmful in two ways, and I've already touched on them, but it's worth the reminder. First, as you journey toward fulfillment in the work you do, you'll bring a fuller and more loving you to your relationship with your son. Second, he's watching every damn move you make. Everything you say and do is likely to be directly reflected in your little boy.

There's a Bible verse that says, "If a son shall ask bread of any of you that is a father, will he give him a stone? Or if he asks a fish, will he for a fish give him a serpent?" That verse goes on to say that if we as men—sinned and flawed and even evil as we are—can give our children good gifts, how much better will the gifts be that are given to those that ask by God the Father.

The part people focus on with that verse is that if man can give his son good things and man is full of sin, then how much more and better will the things be that are given by God. But I want to focus on the first part. It's a presupposition to say that we innately want to give our sons good gifts and feed them good things. Which, unless you're a sociopath or a psychopath, you do want to do.

But the question I want to ask is this: Why are you feeding yourself stones and snakes? In doing so, that's exactly what you're feeding your son. The thing that your heart is most craving is being met with inaction and contentment. You're doing work every day that isn't in line with your gifts or your heart, and you're coming away from it empty and depleted.

If you're eating shit every day, that's what you're feeding your son. And again, unless you're a sociopath or a psychopath, that's not what you want to be doing.

It's what we do with our own lives and the actions we take to make ourselves better by growing that will feed our sons the knowledge and belief and hope that they can do all things.

When you look into your little boy's eyes, you know there are dreams there. There are hopes and big aspirations. The way you cultivate them and not destroy them is to first cultivate and not destroy your own.

THE SCIENCE

The science here is that your life will be significantly shorter if you don't change some habits. You're not a machine, but you can do less of what's easy and more of what's difficult more often than you're doing it now. You'll eventually find that the difficult things become easier when they become habit. You'll think about them less and simply act on them.

> "Within psychology, 'habits' are defined as **actions** that are triggered automatically in response to **contextual cues** that have been associated with their performance." [45]

If you're like me, when you walk into Starbucks, you don't think about or even look at the menu. You just order the drink you order every day, no actual decision-making needed. The *action* is ordering the Venti Dark Roast, and the *contextual cue* is walking into Starbucks. A broader example, if you're a mutant and don't like coffee, is taking a shower before bed. The *action* is taking a shower, and the *contextual cue* is going to bed.

> **"Decades of psychological research consistently show that mere repetition of a simple action in a consistent context leads, through associative learning, to the action being activated upon subsequent exposure to those contextual cues (that is, habitually)."** [45]

The more often we do an action within a specific context, the less we have to think about that action. If my action every time I walk into the kitchen is to grab Cheez-Its and Hot Pockets, because I eat like a five-year-old, then my health will take the hit.

But if I get myself into the rhythm of walking into the kitchen and actually cooking the ground turkey in my fridge that's likely about to be the fourth one to go bad because my current habit is to buy healthy foods without ever actually eating them because I choose Cheez-Its and Hot Pockets instead, then I'll have a healthier experience. Less Hot Pockets equals clearer arteries, even though, they are delicious.

Now, what I just said at the end there is reinforcing the bad habit of eating Hot Pockets because I think they're delicious. But because I'm a realist, I'll say this: they are delicious. Maybe I need to build more habit into my thinking. They are delicious, yes, but I also feel like hell after eating them. Extreme lethargy is the collateral damage, along with other unwanted results, of eating that tasty little croissant filled with cheese and pepperoni. I'm doing a bad job here because now I want a damn Hot Pocket—that cute little pizza shop in a pastry.

> **"Once initiation of the action is 'transferred' to external cues, dependence on conscious attention or motivational processes is reduced. Therefore, habits are likely to persist even after conscious motivation or interest dissipates."[45]**

That's good news because it's hard to motivate myself to cook the ground turkey over eating the Hot Pocket. *wipes sweat from brow*

When I continually just do the action that brings a healthier outcome, I'll have less and less say about the decision. The decision itself dissipates in the presence of the habit. Because of this, I'll eventually be at a place where I have to remind myself that Hot Pockets are, for me at least, a delicious experience and thus have to consciously make the decision to treat myself and eat a Hot Pocket or four from time to time.

There's the key, using the power that's within habit to flip my decision-making around. Now, I have to decide and use cognitive energy to make poorer decisions because my healthier decisions are the ones that are now on autopilot. The healthier actions have now become habit.

Along with this, I can assure you that you will never *feel* like doing the new habits you want to create. You'll never eventually *feel* like having less dopamine rush into your brain after downing a Hot Pocket, some Cheez-Its, and a Coke Zero. So for this to work, you have to choose action over emotion. Keep this graphic in mind when you're reaching for the Cheez-Its or about to hit up the dollar menu:

$$\frac{\text{ACTION}}{\text{EMOTION}}$$

Or you can write it even more simply:

$$\frac{\text{A}}{\text{E}}$$

Choose action over emotion as often as you can, and eventually your day will call on you to make fewer decisions on the things you don't want to be bothered with thinking about. Choosing the action you know you need to take over the emotion that says you don't feel like it will make you successful in literally every aspect of your life. And because much of it becomes habit, your cognitive energy is reserved and can be better spent in other directions, like writing a book to tell dads to kiss their sons.

12

DON'T BE SUCH A GOOD DAD YOU SUCK TO EVERYONE ELSE

This isn't the most comfortable thing to write about. When we tell our stories, we want to be the heroes. We want to be the ones who defeated all our demons. We want to be the ones who faced all the monsters, each scene painted with a villain that we conquered. However, it isn't always like that, and sometimes we're the monster we have to face.

I had been so hyper-focused on being a good dad to Kai for his first almost two years that I totally ignored every other relationship in my life. That's a problem. I caught it before things got totally ruined though, especially with Erin. I'm pretty sure I almost lost Erin. I'm entirely sure that I eventually would have lost Erin if I didn't face some things about myself.

Everybody always talks about growth and that they want to grow and become better, but let me be completely honest with you here—growth is often *fucking painful*. It's beyond uncomfortable. It's disorienting. It calls on you to be more vulnerable than you've ever been or would want to be. Growth requires the death of your old self and the birth of a new one. Neither process is painless.

When I came to the realization that I was letting the fear of being a bad father drive me to be a great father to Kai but run me to the point of being mostly terrible with everyone else around me—including myself by ignoring the things I needed to work through and address—that was a painful realization.

I only wanted to be a great dad to Kai, and I accomplished it and will keep accomplishing it, but I let every other relationship around me wither almost to the point of decay, almost to the point of losing my best friend because she was rightfully sick of me being less than pleasant with every person around me aside from Kai. It turns out that when I was in this overly hyper-focused state toward Kai and succeeding at being a great dad, I wasn't succeeding at being a very good stepdad.

Erin's two children, Cole and Ada, were a little older when I came into the picture, and they have a very present father. Adam, their dad, and I have become good friends, and he and Erin co-parent great together. I think because Cole and Ada have such a present and caring dad, I didn't really see myself as all that necessary to them. And like I mentioned, they were a little older, so they were already kind of in their own rhythm with things before I came along.

I didn't establish bonds with them early on, and by the time Kai was born, I really couldn't be bothered with wanting to create bonds because I was so wrapped up in being a new dad.

I was so completely engulfed in my new role that I truly didn't pick my head up for a second to see what was going on around me—to see what was going on within me. Being a new dad mixed with an ongoing pandemic meant that I didn't want anyone to touch Kai. I would even ask Erin if she washed her hands before I'd hand him to her.

My anxiety at that time was on a whole other level. If I wasn't even sure about Kai's own mom holding him, I sure as hell wasn't letting anyone else get near him without some vicious guard dog-like attitude that was hurtful to those people who loved him. And I didn't care. I was entirely unapologetic about how I was. You do have to take precautions with a newborn, especially in a pandemic, but I became more of a rottweiler. I was just flat-out mean.

There's no greater pain that you can inflict on a mother than when you don't do everything you can to make her children feel valued and cared for, especially when you're their stepfather. Another fucking painful realization. Another moment of shame and embarrassment.

Essentially my relationship with them grew into one of me avoiding interaction with them entirely, and when I would interact with them, I was mostly irritable. When these realizations started to hit me, which was only in the last few months, I immediately got into therapy to address why I was so angry and irritable all the time. And thankfully Cole and Ada are like their mother in being kind and giving me the grace that I really don't deserve.

The other part of this is that they love and show their love for Kai deeply every single day. And he deeply loves them. There's no talk or thought of half-brother or half-sister; it's just brother and sister. So my anger and irritability couldn't find even a glimmer of justification because they've always been incredibly kind and caring toward their little brother. Those three have a sincerely beautiful relationship, and Kai lights up like a thousand Christmas trees when he sees them. When they aren't home and they're with their dad, I can feel how much Kai misses them.

Erin, again rightfully, was sick of me not dealing with the issues I had been promising to deal with for over a year. That included all those issues that I brought into my adult life from that broken distant past as well as my broken recent past— anger, severe anxiety, and insecurity. I had already dealt with the depression successfully by taking medication and utilizing other tools for it. But everything else was left to fester until it became so toxic within me that I almost lost everything.

I knew I had anger that needed to be dealt with, but my only concern was Kai, so everything else could wait. Anger takes a lot of energy, and it really just doesn't feel good to always be filled with anger. It's a shitty state to continually find yourself in. Because I was taking care of Kai and I was so happy when I was with him, I thought all the other stuff could wait. It couldn't.

Couples split up; married or not, it happens. But it might happen less if people were more honest with themselves and made sure that they did absolutely everything they could do to keep the relationship healthy. You can't control your spouse or partner and make them get the help they may need. *You* can only control *yourself*, and *you* have to make sure *you* do everything *you* can to give your children the experience of a healthy home.

Not a perfect home, a healthy home.

This is something to strive for, and there are various studies explaining things like, "Children growing up in homes where two parents have been married continuously are less likely to experience a wide range of problems (academic, social, emotional, cognitive) not only in childhood but later on in adulthood as well."[47] It's not that you just stay together for the kids; it's that you do everything you can to maintain a healthy and vital relationship for them and for you. There are times that it is best for everyone for the relationship to dissolve, but only after every avenue has been explored, every resource exhausted, and every hard truth confronted.

Erin accepted me and loved me immediately when I had less than nothing. All the mess that I was in when we met (bankruptcy, no car, no full-time work, etc.) and my past mess, she accepted without a moment's hesitation.

Erin is the best mom I know, and her kids adore her. Her friends adore and admire her. She's strong and has walked through every challenge life has brought her in stride. She's successful in her business, and though she's strong as an ox, she's gentle, caring, and loving with the people she meets.

She isn't perfect. Our relationship isn't perfect. I'm abundantly imperfect. But I think our imperfections fit together perfectly. Losing her would have been an incredible mistake. I am glad to say that the counseling I've been getting and intend to continue has helped me have a better and growing relationship with Cole and Ada. I see that just because they have a good dad doesn't somehow excuse them or void them from needing a good stepdad.

To you, Cole and Ada: I am sorry, and I do love you both. I really couldn't imagine a better big brother or big sister for Kai to look up to. And I have a pretty good imagination.

Our hearts have amazing and unlimited capacity to love.

UNLIMITED CAPACITY.

You realize the greatness and unending vastness of your heart when you become a parent—you love as if you never loved before and deeper than you ever thought possible. That vastness of love isn't limiting in any way. Maybe I was thinking that if I loved anyone else outside of Kai, like his brother and sister, hell, even his mom, it would somehow take love away from him. What an entirely foolish fear.

Fear is good to a point. It drove me to be better than the things I knew when I was a little boy. But I let it drive me too far, and I almost passed up every other opportunity to love only the way I can uniquely love those around me. Thank God I jumped out of the car before it went over the fucking cliff.

The moment I realized I was about to lose Erin and that I was basically being a piece of garbage to everyone around me, I immediately called the behavioral health center that prescribed me the citalopram for depression and made an appointment to start counseling to address my anger. I had an appointment set up the next day.

Commendable, right?

I took immediate action, right?

Wrong.

Like I mentioned, this was something that I knew I needed to do more than a year prior. I knew these issues needed to be worked through, but I kept putting it off. I knew I was dealing with anger, but since I was good to Kai, it felt like nothing else really mattered.

I thought that I was doing pretty good those first almost two years of being a dad—I finished a master's degree, I had a good job, I was successfully stepping into my new role as a dad (changing diapers, doing late-night feedings, cleaning bottles, being endlessly present and loving to my baby, breaking all those dad stereotypes). I thought I was doing everything right. But when I saw what anger and anxiety and irrational irritability were really doing to me, when I saw how close it was coming to really messing my life up, I realized how much work I needed to do. And I realized I couldn't do it alone.

I didn't lose Erin, thank God. I can love others without losing any capacity to still love my son with everything I am. I realize that love isn't limited or limiting. Quite the opposite. The more love you give, the more love seems to grow within you.

> "'Consider the final words the Buddha
> spoke to his disciples.' 'What's that?'
> I asked, awaiting inspiration.
> 'Just do your best.'"
> —Dan Millman

To those that I hurt because of my anger and unchecked issues, I'm sorry. From here, I can only promise to do my best. And I will.

THE SCIENCE

> "Hundreds of studies have found
> that psychotherapy helps people
> make positive changes in their lives.
> Reviews of these studies show that
> about 75 percent of people who enter
> psychotherapy show some benefit."[46]

Once I confronted the fact that I was dealing with anger problems that were unmanaged and needed managed, I felt shame and embarrassment. I also felt a sense of freedom beginning to emerge, but mostly shame and embarrassment. I wanted to crawl into a hole. I couldn't believe I had let something like that take me so far away from the person I should be.

By the way, this isn't me saying that I'm fully free of that affliction. It's something I've only recently confronted with honesty and began seeking help for. I'm writing about it here because you need to know that it's OK to be a messed-up human who deals with messed-up human things. The sooner we can look honestly at the things in ourselves that we don't want to look at, the sooner we become better for those we love.

If you find yourself, like me, feeling shame and embarrassment, let yourself feel it. Sit in it. Let it wash over you so you can feel how deep the need for change truly is.

I realized that I had some of the worst anger issues on the planet. I never related more to an Avenger than when Bruce Banner said that his secret to transforming into the Hulk at will was that he was always angry. I was always angry. Every day at everything. That was me. And now, I get therapy every other week to quiet it. I still see myself turning green sometimes, but I have more tools and coping strategies to better handle it.

One such tool and strategy is practicing gratitude. Especially in those moments of feeling the pressure rise, I look at the things in my life I'm so incredibly thankful for and meditate on them. I do my best in these moments to replace the angry emotion with feelings of gratitude. Sometimes it works; sometimes it doesn't. I'm human. But it is better than sitting in anger all the time. And I know at the very least, gratitude keeps me sitting in anger for less time than I would be without it. It's a practice, and I'll get better at it. So will you.

Now I feel like the more subdued Professor Hulk that wears glasses. That was when the doctor Bruce Banner and the monster Hulk merged to become a more chilled version of himself. So he's still green and powerful, and likely pissed off, but he has more control over it. That's where I'm at—still green and powerful and pissed off but better able to handle it.

It's realizing that things need to change and seeking help to change them that will be one of the most important things you do in your life. Don't let these things go unchecked, and don't allow pride to keep you from freedom. Even if you don't think your anger is comparable to the Hulk's, talk with someone to see where you might be. Maybe you don't need anything more than a long walk every day to clear your thoughts and burn some anxiety off your chest. Or maybe you need serious therapy and medications. Or you might need all those things. I need all those things plus some. Whatever you need, it's OK. It's OK. Just know that you need it.

> With the use of brain imaging techniques, researchers have been able to see changes in the brain after a person has undergone psychotherapy. Numerous studies have identified brain changes in people with mental illness (including depression, panic disorder, PTSD, and other conditions) as a result of undergoing psychotherapy. In most cases the brain changes resulting from psychotherapy were similar to changes resulting from medication.[48]

This kind of blows my mind. Brain imaging shows that there are actual physical changes happening in the brain as a result of psychotherapy. Alterations in the structure of the brain are occurring because of psychotherapy, and these physical biological changes are similar to the changes seen by taking medications. Psychotherapy is more than just sitting on a couch somewhere crying about our childhood. It's sitting on a couch somewhere crying about our childhood, confronting that trauma and other traumas, exploring truths within that confrontation, and developing practices and exercises to heal ourselves and expand our ability to cope.

> "The medial prefrontal cortex is crucial for the down-regulation of limbic and subcortical regions when subjects are exposed to strong emotions."[49]

> "Cognitive behavioural therapy has been shown to reduce medial prefrontal cortex activity."[49]

> "Reduced activity in the medial prefrontal cortex has been demonstrated after fifteen months of psychodynamic psychotherapy in patients with depression."[49]

The above tells us a story of what's happening biologically to the brain when individuals incorporate psychotherapy with their mental health practices. The part of the brain called the *medial prefrontal cortex* is active in *down-regulating*, which means "slowing down or shutting off," parts of the limbic system in people that have depression, for example.[49]

We've talked about this earlier, but some responsibilities of the limbic system include reward, motivation, and other things we definitely don't feel or experience when we're depressed. Psychotherapy alters the brain in that it causes the activity of the pre-frontal cortex to slow down, which allows the limbic system to do its job—and this allows us to feel the things we'd like to feel when we're walking through depression that we very likely definitely do not feel when we're walking through depression.

> In conclusion, this meta-analysis provides comprehensive evidence that existing psychological and pharmacological interventions are efficacious for improving functioning and quality of life (QoL) in depression. There is no robust evidence that one of the interventions is superior, although psychotherapy appears slightly superior to medication. The combination between psychotherapy and medication performs significantly better for both outcomes when compared to each treatment alone.[49]

This last bit of the research I've looked at shows that there is a higher efficacy rate in quality of life (QoL) and functioning in those who experience depression by doing both psychotherapy and using the right medicine. It shows that psychotherapy alone actually does have a slightly higher efficacy rate than medication alone, but when both are used together, the results are even more effective.

The lesson here . . . cry on the couch and take your meds.

13

DADS, KISS YOUR BABY MOMMAS

Erin and I kiss each other in front of Kai all the time. We kiss Kai relentlessly. When he was an infant, he would get pretty annoyed by us both kissing his cheeks at the same time in rapid succession. Now, he's embraced it and has become an extremely loving little dude.

If I'm holding him, which is often, he'll grab Erin and I and push our faces together so that we kiss and then throw his face in between the kisses. He'll randomly run up to us when he's playing with his toys or watching a movie and plant big wet sloppy kisses all over our faces or foreheads. He's still mostly in the phase where his kisses are drooly and open-mouthed— which was a less painful experience before he had teeth.

I'm really proud of the fact that before he even turned two, he'd openly show his love and affection for the people he cares about. It isn't just Erin and me that get Kai kiss after Kai kiss; it's his aunts, his cousins, his grandparents, his brother, his sister. No one is safe from sloppy wet kisses from Kai.

His hugs are great too. They're always big and warm, and you can feel him fully embracing you—I'm teaching that kid well. There's nothing like loving someone so much that it almost hurts and having that little someone hug and kiss you with everything in them. I have to say it again, I'm so proud of that little boy and how he shows his love for us and everyone he loves.

Our children will reflect the things they see. You and I have to do everything we can to make sure the things they see are the things we want to see reflected in them (read that again). If you show up half of who you are, they'll show up half of who they are. One theme within the pages of this book is to hold, hug, and kiss your little boy. Another very present theme is to do work on yourself so fully that you never show up as half of who you are.

Really sit with that thought. When you find yourself so overcome with this inexplicable love for your little boy, you'll want to bring every piece of your heart with you when you're with him. And bringing every piece of your heart requires it to beat wholly with purpose. Your heart beats wholly with purpose by way of lived, passionate action that's aligned with that purpose that only your heart knows about.

To be whole for your son, you have to be whole. You can't be whole if you're half of who you are. I like keeping things simple. And that's because it is. It's simple to look into your heart and see what brings it to life. It's simple to do the things that bring it to life. It's simple to be whole for your son, who deserves all of you. Don't overcomplicate this. What sets your heart on fire is what you should be doing—so do it. And when your heart's on fire, that flame spreads. There are things you want to ignite in your little boy that can only be done because you ignited them first within yourself.

It takes being bold to look at the life you've been dealt in the past and expect more for the future. There are so many people who believe they're stuck where they are in life because that's where they were born. Answer "yes" to these next questions and allow your current beliefs to shift just an inch in the direction that you want them to go in.

That's the other part of this. Many of us don't even want to believe the beliefs that we believe. We know they're no good and they don't serve us in any way. The only way out of that is to talk against them. When you make even the slightest incremental shift in your belief and act in congruence with it even just a little bit, you'll see how much you can change and how quickly you can change into who you want to be.

Remember, answer "yes" to these questions. Are you bold enough to believe that everything you went through was for something better? Every pain was meant to show you something more about yourself? Every setback was meant to inspire hope? Every letdown meant to inspire expectation? Every single terrible thing you've endured was meant to bring you out on this side of who you are now? Are you bold enough to believe your pain had value and that it hasn't taken away from who you are, but it's actually and beautifully added to who you are? Are you bold enough to be whole by way of your brokenness? Are you bold enough to love as you've never been loved?

Read the questions again audibly out loud and answer "yes" out loud with conviction and as much belief as you can possibly muster. Even if it's the size of a mustard seed.

You're now responsible for what you do with what's been done to you. You have every reason to let the mess of your distant and recent past tear a hole in you, lay down, and bleed out on the floor. But the problem with that is this: PEOPLE FUCKING NEED YOU! Especially your son.

Let that past tear you wide open, but instead of letting it lead to your living death, look inside at what that tear has exposed. That's where your dreams are, that's where your gifts are, that's where your fullness can be found. You've been ripped open so that you can see what's inside. That was the point of the pain. Now, act.

Until you recondition your thinking, you'll always find yourself lost. Until you can find a way to shake the foundation of your current beliefs to make a way for new beliefs, you'll always be stuck. You'll forever repeat the echoes of brokenness that have resounded within your family from one generation to the next.

How do you do it? How do you stop those past echoes of cursed generational patterns and replace them all with newness and life? Keep showing up for yourself. Keep learning. Keep progressing. Keep asking yourself every day if what you're doing is what you want. You've been given an incredible gift. Someone calls you "Dad," and that call awakens and magnifies another calling that's been placed in your heart since you were born. Answer it. Act on it every day.

What our children see is what our children will do.

THE SCIENCE

"A study published by the US Department of Health and Human Services ten years ago found that the quality of a child's parents' marriage had as much influence on his future mental and physical health and well-being as his own relationship with either parent."[51]

Well, damn. That says a lot. That especially speaks to me and how I was those first almost two years of Kai's life when I was ignoring every other relationship around me. I didn't ignore Erin so fully that Kai didn't pick up on becoming the little loving dude that he is, but I could have done better. And I didn't fully realize how important it was to demonstrate love to other people around me instead of only being focused on loving Kai. Like I said, I didn't fully fuck up there, but I could have done better—a lot better in some cases.

> **"And while most parents know how important it is to show love and affection to kids, they can easily overlook that it's critical for the kids to see Mom and Dad love each other, too, especially with the ups and downs and busyness of daily life."[51]**

Well, damn again. I read this article after I'd written most of this book, and if the article hadn't been written in 2019, I'd think someone was staring over my shoulder at Starbucks while I was writing this.

Dads, kiss your sons and kiss your son's mom. To show love to your little boy, show love also to those he loves around him.

It's weird, but sometimes I have to remind myself that Kai loves Erin like his mom—obviously because she is. But to me, she was a girlfriend that became a wife, and I love her, but differently than he does. The thing I have to keep in mind is that he holds her in a very different way within his heart and places an entirely different value on her than I can.

It's not that I value her less, but I certainly value her differently than he does. Now, my reference point of a mom isn't great, at least a biological mom, but I have loved others in my life like a mom. I would only want and *expect* them to be treated with love and respect. That's the expectation Kai holds for me as I interact with his mom. He adores her. He expects the same behavior from me.

This perspective can help you even if you're not in a relationship with your son's mom. Whether you broke up, separated, or divorced, she's his mom. He still holds that adoration and value for her within his heart, and when and if you hurt her, you'll hurt him. Being mindful of who she is in his eyes will help you rethink and rearticulate what you might have otherwise said or done.

This obviously holds relevance if you are still together and in a relationship with your little one's mom. Tony Robbins has a great teaching where he explains to treat your relationship the same way you did when it was new. Treat the relationship like you did when you were just a week out of her swiping right. She isn't just your wife, your girlfriend, or your ex. She's your little boy's mom. Maintain that perspective as best you can.

You'll still fail and say things you don't mean at times, but the more you practice this thought, the more aware you'll become of what's coming out of your mouth. More awareness brings more control. But give yourself some grace by not getting this or anything perfect in your life. Do better. Do your best. With practice, your best starts to become a little better. If you are still together, keep in mind that she's that hot-ass blonde you thought was a bot but was a real human that swiped right. Woohoo!

And if you're not together, remember that your son loves your ex like she's his mom because she is.

Social learning theory suggests that children will imitate the actions they see between their parents. "Therefore, loving and constructive interaction between parents may produce similar behavioral styles in children." *Spillover theory* adds to this by postulating that "emotions or behaviors generated in one family subsystem are transferred to another within the family system."[52]

The love and support that you show to one another are exactly what your son is likely going to imitate in his own life. Those healthy emotions brought about by love and support find their way into the relationship you have with your son and the relationship he has with his mother and the relationships he's going to have with others.

> "Fathers who were more satisfied with
> their current partnership also had a
> better relationship with their infant,
> which in turn was associated with better
> infant personal-social development."[52]

That doesn't mean it's your wife, or your girlfriend, or your ex's job to keep you satisfied, dads. It's simply pointing out that the father-infant relationship is strengthened, and the infant better develops when mom and dad are getting along—more than getting along, sincerely loving and supporting one another. I think that's a key practice here: love and support. When you're loving and supporting the other person, you're putting them ahead of yourself, and when they're loving and supporting you, they're putting you ahead of them. Great things are done when we put each other before ourselves—like our sons growing in an environment filled with the fullness that love and support bring with it. Whether you're happily married or happily unmarried or happily separated or happily divorced, you can still show love and support to one another for the overall benefit of that little one watching every move you make.

It's my responsibility to maturely love and support my son's mother. I know that both relationships—my relationship with Kai and my relationship with Erin—are equivocally valuable and equivocally in need of my time and attention. One is not higher than the other. They are fully in symphony with one another. I cannot have a full relationship with my son if I don't have a full relationship with his mother. Even if we weren't together, it continues to be my responsibility to have as full and supportive of a relationship with her as the circumstance can allow.

> **"Fathers reporting higher levels of depression indicated lower relationship satisfaction, a poorer father-infant relationship, and poorer personal-social development of the infant. Hence, not surprisingly, the postnatal period represents a time of adjustment for fathers, including redefining the relationship and role distributions with their partner and learning to respond adaptively to their infant."**[52]

You may not have ever had to deal with depression, but you have to be brave enough, courageous enough, and bold enough to admit that you may be dealing with it now. No matter how much your partner puts you ahead of themselves or how much you want to put them ahead of you, treating one another with love and support, depression won't allow it.

Depression won't allow you to do these practices that you know will create the environment you wish to create for your little one. This must be fixed first. And you fix it with help.

———

You will not be perfect. You will fight with your son's mom. You will fall short of how you wish yourself to be. And you'll do that much more often than you'd like to. Do your best to find yourself practicing awareness of who this person really is that you're engaging with. And do your best to support and love them, especially when they fail at these same things that you've also failed at, that you'll continue to fail at, and that they'll continue to fail at.

Grace.

Give grace to yourself. Give grace to them.

Love and support as best you can, as often as you can.

14

CHERISHED

The word *cherish* is defined in the *Cambridge Dictionary* in the following way: "to love, protect, and care for someone or something that is important to you." The *Britannica Dictionary* explains *cherish* as, "to feel or show great love for (someone or something)."

I really like that second definition—to show *great* love. *Merriam-Webster* defines *great* as, "remarkable in magnitude and degree." *Merriam-Webster* defines *love* as, "warm attachment, enthusiasm, or devotion." And the example they give is, "love of the sea." I especially like that example because Kai's name means "sea."

What we feel as parents, especially dads, when we hold our babies for the first time, is this great love. In the song I wrote for Kai, the chorus is: "You are my son. You are my great love." To think about the word *great* being "remarkable in magnitude" means that we look at this thing before us in only awe.

We see it with a magnitude and depth that goes further than we can see or imagine. If I could stare at my great love as if it were a thing, it would cover the earth and all the stars of the known and unknown galaxies. It's a sight that I cannot take in wholly with a single gaze. It's a sight that I cannot ever take in wholly because it's ever-expanding.

This is why I tell dads to stick around. Life is hard for everyone. Not a single person has ever gotten out of this thing without some trouble. Even the Bible says shit is gonna get real from time to time. But you and I deserve to experience this other side of life as well. Don't let fear keep you from this. Don't let fear misdirect your steps away from this experience that's so good you'll forget you ever knew heartache.

Stick around, dads. Sit through the unknowing and discomfort so you can come out on the other side fully in love.

And when you come out on this other side, take delight in your son. Even if you're not a God person, this is something from the Bible that I find completely in line with this book. There's a verse in Proverbs 3:12 that says, "The Lord disciplines those he loves, as a father the son he delights in." It's saying that we discipline our sons because we love them. But I want to really focus on the "taking delight in" part of the verse.

Taking delight in my son means I watch him when we're on a walk. I look at his hair and his face and his hands and listen to his voice and his laughter, and I lose myself in it. I take delight in holding Kai and loving him moment through moment. I take delight in looking at his little dino shoes, orange shorts, and tie-dye shirt.

I take delight when I watch his little hand reach out for a snack while we're watching one of his favorite movies—usually *Hubie Halloween*. I take delight in his swooshed-over hair after his bath, his jammies with sharks on them. I take delight especially in his laugh and his smile, his perfect dimples and pearly white teeth. I take full delight in all of who he is.

And it's this delight that leads me to want to make myself better so that I'm as full of a man and a dad as I can be. In doing so, I can better cherish and hold onto all that I'm taking delight in with my son.

Taking delight is the most important practice because it easily leads me to embrace the other practices that ultimately help me take even more delight in him. I don't want to miss even a second of the goodness I get to experience as that little boy's dad.

This is probably the easiest lesson in this book, if you can even call it a lesson. People told me constantly when Kai was first born how fast time would start to speed up. I believed them and took in every ounce of every second that I could. I would just stare at that little baby and let love overflow my heart. Two years later I still do that. I plan on doing it for the rest of my life. This is why, as I've mentioned again and again, it's so important to be doing work that's in line with your purpose.

There's no tug on you to go this way or that way when you've done work that brings you life. You'll be there and present as fully as possible, knowing that the work you did mattered and fell in direct response with your heart's direction. If we aren't listening and acting in the direction of our hearts, they scream louder. The restlessness of an unfulfilled heart will steal you from every moment you want to cherish. The stillness of a heart fulfilled will bring you more presence to the present moment that you want to stay in forever.

Those moments of forever don't last forever. Kai went from newborn infant to wild-ass toddler in what felt like twenty minutes.

And that's coming from someone who's acutely aware of practicing this kind of presence, and it still flew and continues to fly.

I spend many moments in full awareness of those moments with Kai. My point isn't that I'm some enlightened dad-sage. It's that even with my awareness in those moments with my son, the time still races at a blistering speed. Don't figure this thing out too late. You really don't have the time. Work on yourself. Be with your son. Repeat.

THE SCIENCE

> "Mindfulness is a way of directing attention . . . it is generally described as intentionally focusing one's attention on the experience occurring at the present moment in a nonjudgmental or accepting way . . . it has been contrasted with states of the mind in which attention is focused elsewhere, such as preoccupation with memories, fantasies, plans, or worries, and with behaving automatically, without awareness of one's actions."[52]

This preoccupation with plans and other worries is diminished when we live with more discipline in acting on the things we want to do with our lives. As I just mentioned, when we ignore our hearts, they tend to scream louder in the quiet moments we want to be lost in and cherish.

When it's the end of the day and I'm lying in bed with Kai playing games with him on his tablet or rolling on the floor with him wrestling or chasing him around the upstairs and hiding behind doors to jump out at one another, I want to be fully present in those moments. I don't want to be thinking about what I should have done that day. I don't want to be thinking about what I need to do tomorrow because of what I didn't do today. I want to be so fully focused on those moments that when the next morning comes, I can still hear his laugh as clearly as the moment it was happening in.

The first part of that quote says that it's *directing* attention, which means a specific action is required of us. The mind will naturally drift to every possible point of imagination, every past experience (good and bad but usually bad), and every possible future outcome like it's Dr. fuckin' Strange while holding absolutely no interest in the present moment. I think that's because awareness lives in the present moment, and awareness and the mind are separate from one another.

Because of this, it's our responsibility to take on this practice that enriches the time we share with our sons and those we love. I can imagine few things worse than looking back over these last two years and thinking, *I missed it . . .*

Not missing a moment happens by being with the moment. Remember in a previous chapter I said that more awareness brings more control? The more you connect yourself with awareness, the more control you have in experiencing all the goodness that comes from those moments that you know are important. I can see things in those moments that I know I want to hold onto forever. And I'll be able to do it because I'm aware of them. The weight of this is especially so during those first few years when there are so many "firsts" happening.

Another critical piece of this mindfulness practice quoted above is doing it without judgment and with acceptance. For me, this means that you don't beat yourself up when you realize your mind has strayed somewhere else—like, *Is there a vegan option for hotdogs? Should I become vegan? What happens if you Google 'Google'? What's that pain in my side? I'm hungry. Are vegan hotdogs a thing?*

You don't become angry with yourself because your mind is doing what it naturally does. That's like getting mad at rain for being wet. Instead of pulling your mind back to the present like it's a wild dog on a leash, be happy with the peace you find in the realization. Acknowledge that the mind has wandered off, but you then reconnected with awareness to experience the current colorful moment. That's something to be celebrated.

Once the mind goes somewhere else, we don't have to go there ourselves or pull it anywhere. Awareness brings us back because awareness never left. And actually, neither did we, so we're not actually being "brought back" anywhere. Awareness simply snaps us into awareness, and the illusions of the mind, like we're not where we are, turn into smoke.

If we aren't our minds, what are we? I think the answer to that question is that we are awareness itself. Our truest self and awareness must be one in the same. We are consciousness. We are awareness. Those are self. It's the conscious self that follows the mind through its wilderness of ramblings. But when we become aware of our conscious self, which is really just becoming aware of awareness because that is self, then we find peace.

This is also where we find our hearts and connect with them. We can detach from those wilderness ramblings of the mind and allow our authentic self of conscious awareness to bring about the peace of every moment we find ourselves in. We turn from the wilderness ramblings of a madman (the mind) to sitting atop a mountain with the wisest of wisemen (the heart).

When we become aware of our conscious self, we become aware of our conscious self. We wake up. We realize we *are*

conscious awareness, and, in that realization, we aren't bothered by the mind because we experience the mind as separate.
It's here that we're guided by the heart rather than the mind.

> "What a liberation to realize that the 'voice
> in my head' is not who I am. 'Who am I,
> then?' The one who sees that."
> —Eckhart Tolle

We find ourselves stressed when our conscious self has let
go of awareness and depends on the mind for direction. Dan
Millman writes, "Stress happens when the mind resists what
is." Awareness will always accept "what is" because it is fully
conscious of "what is." Awareness and "what is" are one in the
same. There's incredible peace there because resistance resides
somewhere else. Resistance resides within the mind. The mind
will resist "what is" if "what is" is not what the mind would
like it to be. And the mind has no idea what it wishes for
anything to be. The mind is in a constant state of hysterical
spontaneity, which does very little to bring about a result of
peaceful calm and awareness. Awareness does that.

> "I had lost my mind and fallen into my
> heart."
> —Dan Millman

Why put this in the science section of the chapter? Because
science strives for truth. There is no greater truth than conscious awareness of your truest self. You exist right here and

right now. Awareness of your conscious self allows you to realize that. Your mind, however, is on another fucking planet.

Dr. Wayne Dyer often quoted Pierre Teilhard de Chardin, an early twentieth-century French philosopher and priest, saying, "We are not human beings having a spiritual experience; we are spiritual beings having a human experience." The spiritual experience is conscious awareness. The human experience is the mind.

15

DADS, KISS YOUR SONS

I have loved every moment of being a dad. I was fully terrified for most of the months leading up to fatherhood, but those were some of the best months of my life. Erin would likely disagree because the pregnancy was so hard on her. In an earlier chapter I explained that she had hyperemesis gravidarum (HG), which meant she was throwing up literally eight to ten times every single day for eight months straight. There was almost no reprieve from the nausea and vomiting, and I honestly don't know how she made it through. She was never hospitalized for it, and she forced herself to eat and drink and used every ounce of strength she had to keep it down. I mean this when I say it again that she is a fucking warrior. And again, we'll both forever hold close to our hearts that purple bucket that sat next to the bed.

In the few and fleeting moments when Erin was feeling somewhat better, we would go on long walks, about two miles, at the Waterfront—the same place we got married. We'd walk along the river trail almost every day and say hi to the goats that were hired to eat away all the brush and weeds on the hillside. Dale was our favorite goat because he would usually come up to us and follow us as we walked the trail. But after Kai was born, Dale was done with us. I guess he didn't like the competition.

When the eighth month arrived, Erin finally had a break from the HG, but now she wasn't sleeping because the baby was kicking her all night—he's two, and that little shit still doesn't sleep great through the night. Obviously, Erin and I love him like crazy even though we're more than two years into severe sleep deprivation.

I remember so many little things from this time when Erin was pregnant that I'll hold onto forever. I remember taking a picture of her by the river on one of our walks. She was wearing an orange shirt and jean shorts and hated the picture and made me swear to delete it. (I didn't delete it but will probably have to now that she's read this.) I remember putting headphones on her belly and playing classical music—usually Vivaldi or Bach.

I remember her sending me the first ultrasound picture of him waving his hand, at least that's what it looked like, and her writing, "Hi, Dad!" beneath the photo. I remember going to sleep the night before the C-section was scheduled and realizing that we were going to have a baby the next day.

I remember the delivery room. I remember waiting outside the delivery room for what felt like forever and an instant at the same time. I remember hearing him cry. I remember seeing her holding him. I remember them giving him to me. I remember falling in love.

I remember cutting the umbilical cord. I remember falling in love. I remember sitting with him on a rocking chair outside of the delivery room while they got Erin ready to go to our room and the nurses telling me to give him some fatherly advice about life. I remember falling in love. I remember when he held his bottle by himself when he was only two days old. I remember falling in love.

As I watched that little boy sleeping next to his mom last night before I went to bed, I remember falling in love. I fall in love every day, and all I can really remember of these last two years is falling in love over and over and over . . .

Don't miss the greatest thing you can ever remember. Don't miss the greatest love you can ever know. Don't miss it. Dads, kiss your sons.

NOTES

1. Perry, Bruce, D. (2013) "Bonding and Attachment in Maltreated Children: Consequences of Emotional Neglect in Childhood." www.ChildTrauma.org.

2. Porter, Lauren, L. (2003) The Science of Attachment: the Biological Roots of Love. *Mothering,* 119. https://www.naturalchild.org/articles/guest/lauren_lindsey_porter.html.

3. Roxo, M.R., Franceschini, P.R., Zuburan, C., Kleber, F.D., & Sander, J.W. (2011) "The Limbic System Conception and Its Historical Evolution." *The Scientific World Journal,* 11, 2428–2441. https://doi.org/10.1100/2011/157150.

4. Schore, A. N. (2001) "Effects of a Secure Attachment Relationship on Right Brain Development, Affect Regulation and Infant Mental Health." *Infant Mental Health Journal,* 22, 7-66.

5. Dobbing, J. (1997) "Developing Brain Behavior: The Role of Lipids in Infant Formula." *Academic Press.* https://search.ebscohost.com/login.aspx?direct=true&db=nlebk&AN=199036&site=eds-live.

6. Feldman, R. (2017) "The Neurobiology of Human Attachments." *Trends in Cognitive Sciences, 21,* 80-99. https://www.sciencedirect.com/science/article/abs/pii/S1364661316301991?via%3Dihub.

7. Han, Z.R., Gao, M.M., Yan, J., Hu, X., Zhou, W. (2019) "Correlates of Parent-Child Physiological Synchrony and Emotional Parenting: Differential Associations in Varying Interactive Contexts." *Journal of Child and Family Studies*, 28, 1116-1123. https://doi.org/10.1007/s10826-019-01337-4.

8. Nagasawa, M., Okabe, S., Mogi, K., Kikusui, T. (2012) "Oxytocin and Mutual Communication in Mother-Infant Bonding." *Frontiers in Human Neuroscience*, 6, 31. https://doi.org/10.3389/fnhum.2012.00031.

9. Newsbyte. (2021) "The Power of Love—Hugs and Cuddles Have Long-Term Effects." *The Island News*. Retrieved May 18, 2022, from https://yourislandnews.com/the-power-of-love-hugs-and-cuddles-have-long-term-effects/.

10. Pietrangelo, A. (2019) "How Does Dopamine Affect the Body?" *Healthline*. Retrieved May 19, 2022 from https://www.healthline.com/health/dopamine-effects.

11. HealthDirect (2021) "Dopamine." *HealthDirect*. Retrieved on May 19, 2022 from https://www.healthdirect.gov.au/dopamine.

12. Clancy, S. (2008) "DNA Transcription." *Nature Education,* 1, 41. Retrieved May 26, 2022 from https://www.nature.com/scitable/topicpage/dna-transcription-426/.

13. Schwaiger, M., Grinberg, M., Moser, D., et al. (2016) "Altered Stress-Induced Regulation of Genes in Monocytes in Adults with a History of Childhood Adversity." *Neuropsychopharmacol,* 41, 2530-2540. https://www.nature.com/articles/npp201657.

14. Rodriguez-Esteban, R., Jiang, X. (2017) "Differential Gene Expression in Disease: A Comparison Between High-Throughput Studies and Literature." *BMC Med Genomics*, 10, 59. https://bmcmedgenomics.biomedcentral.com/articles/10.1186/s12920-017-0293-y.

15. Bollati, V., Baccarelli, A. (2010) "Environmental Epigenetics." *Heredity*, 105, 105-112. https://www.nature.com/articles/hdy20102.

16. Centers for Disease Control and Prevention. (2022, May 18). "What Is Epigenetics?" *Centers for Disease Control and Preven-*

tion. Retrieved May 27, 2022, from https://www.cdc.gov/genomics/disease/epigenetics.htm.

17. *Etymology*. (n.d.). Retrieved May 27, 2022, from https://www.etymonline.com/word/epi- .

18. Cuncic, A. (2020) "What Exactly Is Psychopathology?" *Verywell Mind*. Retrieved May 28, 2022, from https://www.verywellmind.com/an-overview-of-psychopathology-4178942.

19. Friedrich, M. (2017) "Depression Is the Leading Cause of Disability Around the World." *JAMA, 317*, 15. Retrieved June 2, 2022, from https://jamanetwork.com/journals/jama/article-abstract/2618635.

20. World Health Organization. (2021) "Depression." *World Health Organization*. Retrieved June 2, 2022, from https://www.who.int/news-room/fact-sheets/detail/depression.

21. Stringaris, A. (2017) "Editorial: What Is Depression?" *The Journal of Child Psychology and Psychiatry, 58*, 1287-1289. Retrieved June 2, 2022, from https://acamh.onlinelibrary.wiley.com/doi/pdf/10.1111/jcpp.12844.

22. Levinson, D. F., & Nichols, W. E. (n.d.). "Major Depression and Genetics." *Genetics of Brain Function*. Retrieved June 3, 2022, from https://med.stanford.edu/depressiongenetics/mddandgenes.html.

23. US Department of Health and Human Services. (2022). "Suicide." *National Institute of Mental Health*. Retrieved June 3, 2022, from https://www.nimh.nih.gov/health/statistics/suicide.

24. OCDUK. (n.d.). "How SSRIs Work." Retrieved June 3, 2022, from https://www.ocduk.org/overcoming-ocd/medication/how-ssri-work/.

25. Zhong, Z., Wang, L., Wen, X., Liu, Y., Fan, Y., & Liu, Z. (2017). "A Meta-Analysis of Effects of Selective Serotonin Reuptake Inhibitors on Blood Pressure in Depression Treatment: Outcomes from Placebo and Serotonin and Noradrenaline Reuptake Inhibitor Controlled Trials. *Neuropsychiatric Disease and Treatment, 13*, 2781–2796. https://doi.org/10.2147/NDT.S141832.

26. Wax, D. (2021). "The Science of Setting Goals (and Its Effect on Your Brain)." *Lifehack*. Retrieved June 11, 2022, from https://www.lifehack.org/articles/featured/the-science-of-setting-goals.html.

27. Feldman, D., Rand, K., Kahle-Wrobleski, K. (2009). "Hope and Goal Attainment: Testing a Basic Prediction of Hope Theory." *Journal of Social and Clinical Psychology,* 28(4), 479-497.

28. Berkman E. T. (2018). The Neuroscience of Goals and Behavior Change." *Consulting Psychology Journal,* 70(1), 28–44. https://doi.org/10.1037/cpb0000094.

29. Chowdhury, M. R. (2022). "The Science & Psychology of Goal-Setting 101." *PositivePsychology.com*. Retrieved June 12, 2022, from https://positivepsychology.com/goal-setting-psychology/.

30. Reupert, A., Straussner, S.L., Weimand, B., Maybery, D. (2022). "It Takes a Village to Raise a Child: Understanding and Expanding the Concept of the 'Village.'" *Frontiers in Public Health.* 10, 1-7. Retrieved June 21, 2022 from https://www.frontiersin.org/articles/10.3389/fpubh.2022.756066/full#B27.

31. Haslam, C., Cruwys, T., Haslam, S. A., & Jetten, J. (2015). "Social Connectedness and Health." *Encyclopedia of Geropsychology,* 1–10. https://doi.org/10.1007/978-981-287-080-3_46-1.

32. Pattakos, A. (2021). "Guiding Yourself and Others to Meaning." *Psychology Today.* Retrieved June 29, 2022, from https://www.psychologytoday.com/us/blog/the-meaningful-life/202106/guiding-yourself-and-others-meaning.

33. Yaribeygi, H., Panahi, Y., Sahraei, H., Johnston, T. P., & Sahebkar, A. (2017). "The Impact of Stress on Body Function: A Review." *EXCLI Journal,* 16, 1057–1072. https://doi.org/10.17179/excli2017-480.

34. Reznikov LR, Grillo CA, Piroli GG, Pasumarthi RK, Reagan LP, Fadel J. (2007). Acute Stress-Mediated Increases in Extracellular Glutamate Levels in the Rat Amygdala: Differential Effects of Antidepressant Treatment." *European Journal of*

Neuroscience. 25:3109–3114. https://doi.org/10.1111/j.1460-9568.2007.05560.x.

35. Bremner, J. D. (1999). "Does Stress Damage the Brain?" *Biological Psychiatry.* 45(7), 797-805. https://doi.org/10.1016/S0006-3223(99)00009-8.

36. Rozanski, A., Blumenthal, J., Kaplan, J. (1999). "Impact of Psychological Factors on the Pathogenesis of Cardiovascular Disease and Implications of for Therapy." *Circulation.* 99(16), 2192-2217. Retrieved on July 12, 2022 from https://www.ahajournals.org/doi/full/10.1161/01.CIR.99.16.2192.

37. Moran, E., Bradshaw, C., Tuohy, T., & Noonan, M. (2021). "The Paternal Experience of Fear of Childbirth: An Integrative Review." *International Journal of Environmental Research and Public Health*, *18*(3), 1231. https://doi.org/10.3390/ijerph18031231.

38. Darwin, Z., Galdas, P., Hinchliff, S., Littlewood, E., McMillan, D., McGowan, L., Gilbody, S., & Born and Bred in Yorkshire (BaBY) team (2017). "Fathers' Views and Experiences of Their Own Mental Health During Pregnancy and the First Postnatal Year: A Qualitative Interview Study of Men Participating in the UK Born and Bred in Yorkshire (BaBY) Cohort." *BMC Pregnancy and Childbirth*, 17(1), 45. https://doi.org/10.1186/s12884-017-1229-4.

39. Kolala, R. (2020). "The Roots of Chemistry: How the Ancient Tradition of Alchemy Influenced Modern Scientific Thought." *The Aggie Transcript.* Retrieved July 25, 2022, from https://aggietranscript.ucdavis.edu/the-roots-of-chemistry-how-the-ancient-tradition-of-alchemy-influenced-modern-scientific-thought/.

40. Kane, L. (2014). "9 Things Rich People Do And Don't Do Every Day." *Business Insider.* Retrieved July 28, 2022, from https://www.businessinsider.com/rich-people-daily-habits-2014-6.

41. Gelles-Watnick , R., & Perrin, A. (2021). "Who Doesn't Read Books in America?" *Pew Research Center.* Retrieved July 28, 2022, from https://www.pewresearch.org/fact-tank/2021/09/21/who-doesnt-read-books-in-america/.

42. Renzetti, Claire M. (2009). "Economic Stress and Domestic Violence." *Center for Research on Violence Against Women Faculty Research Reports and Papers*. 1. https://uknowledge.uky.edu/crvaw_reports/1.

43. "Special Heart Risks for men." *Johns Hopkins Medicine*. (2021). Retrieved July 29, 2022, from https://www.hopkinsmedicine.org/health/wellness-and-prevention/special-heart-risks-for-men.

44. Centers for Disease Control and Prevention. (2022). Men and Heart Disease. *Centers for Disease Control and Prevention*. Retrieved July 29, 2022, from https://www.cdc.gov/heartdisease/men.htm#:~:text=About%201%20in%2013%20(7.7,men%20have%20coronary%20heart%20disease.&text=Half%20of%20the%20men%20who,disease%20had%20no%20previous%20symptoms.&text=Even%20if%20you%20have%20no,at%20risk%20for%20heart%20disease.

45. Gardner, B., Lally, P., & Wardle, J. (2012). "Making Health Habitual: The Psychology of 'Habit-Formation' and General Practice." *The British Journal of General Practice: The Journal of the Royal College of General Practitioners*, *62*(605), 664–666. https://doi.org/10.3399/bjgp12X659466.

46. American Psychological Association. (n.d.). "Understanding Psychotherapy and How It Works." *American Psychological Association*. Retrieved August 9, 2022, from https://www.apa.org/topics/psychotherapy/understanding.

47. "40 Facts About Two Parent Families: Studies and Statistics." *GillespieShields*. (2020, February 28). Retrieved August 3, 2022, from https://gillespieshields.com/40-facts-two-parent-families/.

48. "What Is Psychotherapy?" *Psychiatry.org* (n.d.). Retrieved August 8, 2022, from https://psychiatry.org/patients-families/psychotherapy.

49. Kamenov, K., Twomey, C., Cabello, M., Prina, A. M., & Ayuso-Mateos, J. L. (2017). "The Efficacy of Psychotherapy, Pharmacotherapy and Their Combination on Functioning and Quality of Life in Depression: A Meta-Analysis." *Psycho-

logical medicine, 47(3), 414–425. https://doi.org/10.1017/ S0033291716002774.

50. Villines, Z. (2019, March 14). "6 Ways the Limbic System Impacts Physical, Emotional, and Mental Health." *GoodTherapy. org Therapy Blog*. Retrieved August 9, 2022, from https://www. goodtherapy.org/blog/6-ways-the-limbic-system-impacts-physical-emotional-and-mental-health-0316197.

51. Swindell Day, S. (2019). "Yes, You Should Be Affectionate in Front of the Kids!" *Nashville Parent*. Retrieved August 16, 2022, from https://nashvilleparent.com/yes-you-should-hug-in-front-of-the-kids/.

52. Baer, R. (2014). "Mindfulness-Based Treatment Approaches." *Academic Press*.

ABOUT THE AUTHOR

 Mark Craven is the author of several books and writes a self-development blog for his website, www.SuccessUpAhead.com. Mark also hosts the podcast, *The Craven Effect*. He has worked as a Math Instructor, Student Success Coach, and Senior Academic Advisor at the college level. He holds a bachelor's degree in Biology and a master's degree in Higher Education Management. Mark lives in Pittsburgh, Pennsylvania with his family.

GET THESE TITLES BY MARK CRAVEN

BLOG BOOK VOL. 2:
The Demons I Meet

BLOG BOOK VOL. 1:
We Shouldn't Have Met This Soon

KARYEATOR

TWO-STEP SUCCESS

BE A HERO TO YOUR HEART

CHOICE AND TRIUMPH

SUBSCRIBE TO THE PODCAST!

THE CRAVEN EFFECT

MARK CRAVEN

A podcast about connecting!

Available on these platforms:

Anchor Apple Google Breaker Castbox Overcast Pocket Radio Stitcher Spotify
Podcasts   Casts Public

JOIN THE NEWSLETTER AT
WWW.DADSKISSYOURSONS.COM

9 798987 769201